Choosing JOY

Choosing JOY

Change Your Life for the Better

by
Gary Null
with
Vicki Riba Koestler

Carroll & Graf Publishers, Inc.
New York

First Carroll & Graf edition 1998

Carroll & Graf Publishers, Inc.
19 West 21st Street
New York, NY 10010

Library of Congress Cataloging
in Publication Data is available.
ISBN: 0-7867-0522-1

Manufactured in the United States of America

Contents

Choosing JOY

How To Use This Book

Most of us know that life is a journey, but at any given stage of life, we may not have a clear perspective on where we are on the road to personal growth—emotionally, spiritually, intellectually and physically. *Choosing Joy* is designed to help you determine where you are today and what you need to do to achieve personal fulfillment.

As you read through each section, you will be asked to consider a wide variety of questions about your life. The objective is to delve into your personal experiences, identify your true needs and discover what is meaningful to you. This process will require you to think through many of your life experiences, both negative and joyful. It will encourage you to see who you really are so that you can express that self to the world.

Keep a pen and a notebook with you as you use this book and take the time to make written notes of your answers to the questions. There is room to jot down notes and lists on the margins of the pages. For more detailed answers, keep a journal. You will find that the questions which are most meaningful to you will stimulate you to write your ideas at length.

I believe that writing about yourself is indispensable to

personal development. By making the time to keep a journal, and thinking through what you plan to write, you will stimulate the process of growth and change. With every question you consider, you set into motion a dialogue with your inner self. It is a purely introspective process—one that honestly reflects your feelings without the interference of outside influences. This is not to say that other approaches to self expression, such as talking to a counselor or a friend, are not viable as well. However, I truly believe that the first step toward personal development is to get in touch with your own feelings. After all, no one knows you as well as you know yourself.

I have provided a short discussion of issues raised by each question you are asked to answer. These comments reflect my subjective view; hence, they are not necessarily "correct" from your perspective. The discussions are meant to stimulate your thought processes. In the end, however, you must get in touch with your feelings and your own personal truth.

Throughout this book I ask you to assess both your positive and negative qualities. To benefit from the process, you must be honest with yourself. Only then will you be able to eliminate negative behavior and identify the positive attributes that deserve more of your time and energy. This process, in turn, will allow you to steer your life in a more constructive direction.

The process of personal growth is certainly not easy. What's easy is to lose sight of your real needs, stagnate in your growth, and experience more of the same each day. It takes courage, resolve and a commitment of time and energy to make positive changes in your life and stimulate your growth. It is hard but ultimately rewarding work, and I welcome you to the challenge.

Introduction

The day of my high school graduation was one of the saddest days of my life. After hats were thrown into the air I came to the somber realization that nothing would ever be the same again. I had been friends with many of these people for most of my 18 years, and we were supposed to be friends for life. But in spite of childhood promises, I knew my friendships would suddenly evaporate after graduation day.

That night we all made the rounds, as in the movie *American Graffiti*, driving past our old haunts. I committed each smiling face that I encountered to memory. Despite the party atmosphere, my underlying feeling was morbid, as if I were looking into a casket and saying good-bye for the very last time. It was not a happy night.

When I arrived home, it was four o'clock in the morning. I was surprised to see my dad sitting on the steps waiting for me. He was a man who had a bittersweet existence, a brilliant man who, to my mind, was more innovative and progressive than it was comfortable for his friends and associates to acknowledge. Instead of receiving encouragement, he got negative feedback from the important people in his life. He tried to fit into society by acquiescing to its demands and expectations, and in the process suppressed his true spirit. Eventually he began to drink as a way of drowning out the creative part of his psyche. He never fell down drunk, but all of my life he was belligerent, angry, and blaming.

On this night, however, he was not drinking. He was sitting there waiting for me, something he had never done before.

I asked, "What are you doing up, Dad? It's four o'clock in the morning."

He replied, "I realize there were many times in your life I should have helped you to understand how life changes, but I didn't and I'm sorry." He paused for a moment, then looked me square in the eye and went on, "My graduation from high school was one of the saddest days of my life because I knew things would never be the same again. I knew that everyone who had accepted me and supported my ideas would be gone. Childhood friendships would be over, along with feelings of being able to master anything. Even though we had different economic and cultural backgrounds, we all believed in our equal ability to do anything we set our minds to. But once we left school, everything changed."

I told him that was very strange because all day I had been having similar feelings. I had been acknowledged all these years for expressing myself through poetry, athletics, and essays, and for standing up to things I felt were unjust in society—but now I wasn't going to have anyone else's support.

He agreed that my perceptions were correct. Then he gave me some important advice.

"I want to share something with you that may give you a completely different view of life," my father said. "I want you to do something that I didn't do, Gary Michael. I want you to leave this community. This was a wonderful place to spend your childhood. There is innocence and honesty here, as well as the spirit of adventure and exploration. You were never told you couldn't do things. You were always encouraged, even when you climbed out your window at night and slid down the drainpipe right past your mother and me in the kitchen. We knew you were going out to build your tree house, but we didn't stop you.

"Another time you took your lunch box and went out for five hours to see if you could find the end of the rainbow. You were only five years old, but determined to find it. We let you walk all the way to the end of town, cross the bridge that separates West Virginia from Ohio, and go into the countryside ten miles away. We wanted you to know that you might not find the end of the rainbow, but it was worth looking for. You should always believe that you could. We felt it was important for you to have the sense that there is something out there for you, something more than the eye can see."

Before that talk, I never thought of all the positive values my parents had instilled in me. By allowing me the opportunity to explore life early, they encouraged me to be idealistic. I learned that honest people can be powerful and that systems are there to help, not to limit us.

As a child, I was allowed to see, hear, and speak to imaginary friends, and this taught me to be open to myriad possibilities in life. Had I been discouraged from believing in gods and goddesses, inner guides and inner spirits, it would have quickly stilled my childlike innocence. It would have taught me to accept only the materialistic processes of life and to distrust natural ones.

My father taught me to believe that I was connected to

something larger than life and to question convention. Although I was raised as a Baptist, I was not afraid to challenge tradition. I was the only young person in church, for example, ever to stand up in front of the entire congregation and ask the embarrassed minister how we ended up with blacks and Chinese and other people in the world if Adam and Eve were the only two people ever created.

If my parents hadn't let me have those experiences, and if my father hadn't summed it up for me that night, I might have felt limited by the things I had not been allowed to do. Perhaps I would have broken away from them rebelliously so that I could do all the things they had prevented me from doing. Instead of learning that I could challenge old systems or make new ones, I might have fallen into line with everyone else.

My father then gave me his car keys for the first time. He wanted me to use the car to visit my friends and see that something had changed. I appreciated that and I gave him a hug. I told him how I was touched by his sharing this transition I was going through because it was lonely and terrifying. I had no idea what tomorrow would bring, but I knew it would be different.

"Leave this town as soon as you can and start your journey in life," my father repeated. He told me that my upbringing had been a preparation for my journey. He believed that it prepared me to leave home with a sense of integrity; it gave me patience and a work ethic. It gave me the confidence to make a life for myself, not just a living. It taught me to share, rather than manipulate others, and helped me avoid competing for the wrong reasons—just to win, to prove myself right, or to engage in personal power plays. It kept me from being argumentative just to keep control of a conversation. Importantly, it kept me from denigrating women. My dad had tried to keep any of those negative qualities from being instilled in me.

"Don't ever let anyone tell you that your values are implausible, naive, stupid, or impractical," Dad warned. "And believe me, they'll try because they have lost their vision and have become cynics. I don't want you to end up like me, Gary Michael," he went on. "When I was 17 years old, I was just like you. But I did not hold to my principles. No matter what happens, hold on to your principles."

The next day I took my father's car and went around to see all my friends. Just 24 hours earlier, we had been talking about things we wanted to do together. Now they were all too busy for me.

"Hi, Tim, want to go swimming?"

"I can't, Gary. Got to work in Dad's shop."

"Do you know when you can get free? Do you want to go fishing this weekend?"

"I can't, Gary."

"We've got a whole summer ahead."

"I'm going to be working all summer. Playtime's over. Got to grow up now. Got to take things seriously."

Every single person I visited said almost the same thing. I was faced with something I'd never seen before—the death of passion and desire. It was as if I had entered a town of Stepford wives. At the end of the day, I realized my father was right. To stay in town would mean conforming and surrendering all of my high aspirations. A new journey was about to begin.

I went to New York City with nothing but $53 in my billfold and it was stolen the first day. Luckily I had another $12 in my pocket for emergencies. That and a positive attitude kept me going. I remembered that no matter what environment I was in, I should look for things that allowed me to feel good about myself. I refused to acknowledge the fact that I had no money. I slept sitting up in the bus station for three nights before finding work as a short-order cook. At least that gave me a place to eat. Then I found a YMCA that cost only $2.50 a night, and moved in.

That was my introduction to my new life. The beginnings were difficult and frightening but the results have been very rewarding. I now appreciate more than ever those lessons of growth and change. I understand that we are here on this earth to manifest a higher character and consciousness by continuing to use every event, crisis, and problem as another lesson of how to make better choices and how to respond to them when we realize we've made the wrong ones. I cannot always create my own reality but I can choose how I want to respond to it.

I struggled to succeed many times in my life. I never stopped, even when my first book was rejected 130 times in two years and my income was less than $5000 a year. I never lost faith that one day I would succeed because I continued to seek the end of the rainbow. Sometimes I wonder what would have happened had I stopped at the second rejection or the eighth, when the editor added a little letter to the standard rejection form that read, "You'd best find another profession. Clearly writing is not your forte." That, coupled with the fact that I was so poor I couldn't even mail my manuscripts to publishers, could have easily discouraged me. But I never got angry. I never felt deprived. I took advantage of everything worthwhile that was free—outdoor concerts and plays, book forums and poetry readings, wonderful walks in the park, nice company and stimulating conversations, and especially the old New Yorker bookstore, a landmark in New York City, where I could read a book a day without having to buy one. Then one day a publisher liked my ideas and published my first book.

When I first decided to racewalk I was determined to succeed even though I was less than promising at the start. In the first race I entered there were more than 75 racewalkers, and of everyone racing I was dead last. People in their 70s walked faster than I did. In fact, I was so slow that no one realized I was still on the course. By the time I finished, the winners had received their awards and gone home. Someone came over to me and said, "What are you doing in this race?" I replied, "I'm learning." Winning wasn't important. I did it to learn, and anything I learned was going to be to my advantage.

It would be almost a year before I would understand enough about form, style, and proper training to be able to improve substantially, but my determination paid off. Recently, I was given an award for my achievements—Outstanding Track and Field MAC Master Champion Athlete of the Year. I've also won the indoor grand prix series for all athletes of all ages and all categories. That's the first time in history that a racewalker has won either of those two coveted prizes. I now hold many personal meet, course, and national records and have won more than 100 championships. What if I had thought of quitting in my first, fifth, or twentieth race when I came in last?

When I first started in broadcasting I worked from a tiny radio station where the listenership couldn't have been more than 100 or 200 people. The owner of the station openly discouraged me from doing more shows. He told me, "You don't have a radio voice."

To this I replied, "Why, because I have a soft voice and don't yell?"

"That's right," he said. "You have to have a hyperkinetic voice that excites and interests people."

"What if I share something of interest?" I questioned. "Does the announcer always have to be the main focus? Why not the message he's delivering?"

He didn't understand this and told me that I shouldn't be on the radio because I was talking about health and no one was interested.

But I didn't quit. I kept on. I was told that I couldn't syndicate a show, but I did. And I ended up in the top markets in prime time. Then I was told that I couldn't succeed on a noncommercial radio station, WBAI—The Pacifica Foundation. Not only have I succeeded, I've been there 20 years with one of the longest-running daily talk shows on noncommercial radio, uninterrupted, in American history.

The same story holds true for my other achievements—writing articles, doing scientific research, earning two doctorates. I always began in last place. I started with many disadvantages and a lot of negative feedback from all the naysayers.

I learned from these experiences to surround myself with positive people who have kind hearts and who are spiritually and emotionally healthy. There was a time I didn't do that. I thought that people would change if you were kind to them. But people who are negative are determined to bring you down with them and can only hurt your progress. Learning when to let go of such people is very important to your personal growth.

A few years ago I attended my twentieth high school reunion. It was a disturbing experience. My old classmates all looked older than their years to me as I went from table to table and asked them what they had been doing in the past 20 years. I was surprised at their answers. "Not a whole lot." "Nothing." "Just working." I didn't hear anyone talk about having fulfilled their dreams or even having looked for the rainbow. Many had been divorced two or three times and were angry and unfulfilled, almost bitter about life.

I was surprised, however, that many of them had kept track of my career and had occasionally seen me on television. But none of them had read any of my books or had actually followed a health program. None had travelled to Europe or other far-off places. Most had stayed close to home their entire lives. Some said they were happy, but not many.

I felt very sorry for my old classmates and sad that the next time I would see most of them would be at their funerals. These people had gone from the bright horizons of childhood, when they believed everything was possible, to the narrow and limiting concepts of an adulthood in which they believed they could do only what they were told to do. They had lived their lives without ever having fulfilled any of their dreams. Even those who had gone to college fell back into the old routines when they returned, joined the family business and lived in the old hometown.

I found the whole event depressing. But several months afterwards my perception of what I had seen at the reunion began to change. That was because I was starting to develop the concept of natural life energies, the idea that a person is driven predominantly by one of seven different types of energy. For instance, a Dynamic Aggressive is someone driven to organizing enterprises, thinking on the grand scale, and, in the process, delegating the day-to-day details to other people. The Adaptive Assertive, on the other hand, can be a detail person par excellence. The Creative Assertive is by innermost nature an artist of some sort, and the Adaptive Supportive, by contrast, is generally not impelled to create something new but rather to follow others' leads and enjoy a routine. Other energy types are the Adaptive Aggressive, the Dynamic Assertive, and the Dynamic Supportive. These are all described in depth in my book *Who Are You Really?: Understanding Your Life's Energy*, but the point here is that I hadn't been taking the differences in people's energy types into account.

As a result, my expectations about how my old high school friends should have been living their lives had been based too much on how I was conducting mine. As a Dynamic Assertive, I had been driven all my life by a love of ideas, specifically, of new ideas, ones that I could develop and explain to others, and then develop some more. I liked to push the envelope of what was generally accepted or even imagined, and, as an energy type that could get pushy and radical and be seen as a pain in the neck by more conventional folks, there was a good chance I would not have been happy staying in a small town after high school. My father was a Dynamic Assertive too, I now saw. That was why he'd been so adamant about my leaving town on graduation night. He himself had been constrained by the town's limited range of vision, and he didn't want me to experience the same life of feeling held in at every turn. I hadn't understood his foresight so clearly before.

I also hadn't seen that there is an energy type that actually thrives staying in the old neighborhood for a lifetime, and that's the Adaptive Supportive. People whose hearts are centered on their extended family, and who appreciate knowing what to expect each day in the workplace, have no need to emigrate from their home base nor seek exciting jobs. Creative Assertives can do well in small towns too, as can Dynamic

Supportives, especially after people with these energies have spent some years away in the big city. Then they can return and happily continue doing what matters to them—honing their craft or helping people, respectively. In short, I had to revise my conclusion that most everyone I'd seen at that reunion was miserable. Maybe the majority who'd insisted that they were happy really *were*. Maybe many who looked utterly defeated were just tired. Not that I accept looking totally spent in one's 40's, but there's a difference there, and I had to revise my judgment about my old classmates.

A strange point for a writer of a book like this to be making—that he'd had to revise his opinion, and recently too! But it's an important point. I'm not the authority. I'm not any smarter or more infallible than you are. This book is written mostly in a question-and-answer format, and there's a reason for that: Although I give my personal answers to the questions, you're supposed to come up with your own too, and if they're different from mine, or go beyond mine, so much the better. I'm a Dynamic Assertive, I can handle it! And seriously, the whole idea behind the book is to get you to think about important life issues, not to accept what I believe, necessarily.

All that said, I do still feel that many people at my high school reunion, and many that I encounter every day, are capable of having more joy in their lives than they have at present. That's why I wrote this book. In counseling people I get frustrated because I believe that most people don't realize how very close they are to fulfillment. So many fall into the trap of thinking their life would be better if their circumstances were different. They wonder what would happen if they had been born wealthy instead of middle class or poor, if they had inherited greater athletic skills or more intellect. They think about what it would be like to have been born male instead of female or vice versa, or to have been born in Manhattan instead of Minnesota, or vice versa there too. They also look to others to save them. Politicians will give them a better quality of life, they believe. Doctors will keep them healthy. Teachers will make them smarter. Psychologists will make them feel better. Spiritual gurus will show them the way. Or so they think.

In this book I want to share a different perspective, one that may require you to rethink your assumptions about life, just as I have. Consider the following: *What if the things you thought were causing your problems really weren't? What if the problems didn't exist out there, but rather in you?*

Suddenly, with this perspective, life gets simpler, easier. Outside obstacles to doing what you want to do and being what you want to be begin to fall away, and you see that you have more choices—positive ones.

That's what this book is about—the positive things that you can start doing—right now. The chapter titles tell it all: becoming the hero in your own life, creating contentment, beating self-defeating habits, choosing joy. All of these are positive choices you can make if you drop the blaming-others, blaming-circumstances strategy and concentrate on your own strengths and sense of purpose. The idea behind this book is to help you find these, and, if you already have, to join with you in celebrating life's potential.

Making Life Simple Again

1

Most of us can remember simpler times. Life was less complex, was filled with fewer responsibilities, and seemed to contain more time. Many baby boomers today are examining their lives and finding themselves materially affluent but seemingly time-poor. After years of focusing on careers, families, and the accumulation of the "right" things, they're beginning to ask themselves what all the striving and rushing around are about. Many are now seeking ways to live less stressful lives, and not just on vacation or during a weekend. They want to live with a consistent sense of peace. This can be hard, though, after many years of daily turmoil.

In fact, most Americans have difficulty relaxing. They don't know how to unwind, and even find the process of unraveling on a vacation or a retreat to be stressful. I can tell you that from my experiences with people who have come down to my ranch in Texas. The first three days I have to give lots of workshops. I keep my guests busy all day because if there's a free moment, they panic and wonder, "Where should I go now?" "What should I do?"

By the end of the week, people are finally able to relax, and they don't need all the workshops. Instead, they want to spend more time by themselves, with the animals, with nature.

People could relax sooner if they could learn how to leave their problems and anxieties behind, to live in the moment. Living in the moment has become a cliché associated with the New Age movement. But what does it really mean, and how can we get there? First of all, what keeps us from being in the moment and how does that affect us?

Are you aware of the factors that keep you from fully experiencing the present?

Avoidance

How can you be in the moment if you are avoiding what you need to do? When you distract yourself from the task at hand, you are not allowing the moment to happen. When two things compete for your attention, neither one has it fully. You avoid going to the dentist, for example, because you have an abscess and you are afraid. You distract yourself from the pain by watching television. You focus all your energy away from the problem. That keeps you out of the moment.

Rushing

Do you rush to avoid being late, even if you have plenty of time? In the process of worrying about being prompt, you create stress that prevents you from enjoying the moment. You lose touch with your natural rhythm. Going someplace in a hurry is a forced, highly aggressive state. You become hyper.

The moment is lost because you have allowed your mind to be someplace that your body is not. You are not comfortable with where your body is; you want it to be someplace else.

You feel that you are going to be judged. Why else would you be concerned about being someplace on time? Or you are judging yourself so that someone else won't judge you. Being harsh on yourself is a defense mechanism in that you hope that by judging yourself, you'll avoid the criticism of others. After all, it's hard to beat up on someone emotionally if they've already beaten up on themselves! So we make sure we do a pretty good job of it.

Anticipating Others' Anger

What would happen if you decided to change how you dealt with other people's anger? What if you decided their anger was their business and not yours? What if you decided not to process it? Even if there is value and legitimacy in what they are angry about, the emotion is theirs to process. You don't have to clutter up your life with it. The moment you take on someone else's anger, you take on all of the negativity that comes with it.

Being Angry Ourselves

When we ourselves are angry, the emotion often prevents us from dealing with important issues. Frequently, it's born out of frustration. We feel that systems are too insensitive and corrupt to change. Anger, then, is used as a substitute for action. In effect, we are saying, "I am powerless to do anything." If we give up at that point, we deprive ourselves from affecting the moment. Then our time to be constructive is gone.

Is what you do guided by what you believe?

When I get up in the morning, I know that whatever I'm going to do that day will honor my life, and my basic beliefs. It's the same every single day, which in a sense makes life extremely simple. My personal morality is a constant.

Never do I compromise on my principles. I was once offered a deal in which I was to receive $50,000 for endorsing a junk food product filled with sugar. I refused to do it even though I didn't have any money at the time. They tried hard to convince me to do the endorsement. They pointed out, "If you don't do this, Gary, another nutritionist will." They were right. Another nutritionist did.

I called that other nutritionist, and I asked, "You're not going to endorse this product, are you?"

He replied, "Why shouldn't I? It's $50,000."

"But it's not a good product," I said.

"There's a lot of not good products around," he retorted. "It's all relative. People can take some vitamins along with the stuff, so what's the big deal?"

I said, "That's like beating someone up and apologizing at the same time. Why beat them up to begin with?"

He pretended he didn't understand.

Then I started looking around, and I saw people everywhere making major compromises. Sometimes people do this to make money. And sometimes they do it to avoid feeling alienated. When you stand up and say how you feel, there's a chance others are not going to like you. Particularly if you're the one bringing unhappy tidings about wrongdoings, you're not going to be liked, and you're certainly not going to be accepted.

On the other hand, if you get into the habit of living

honestly, you're going to like yourself. You'll be relieved of the burden of self-doubt and of the vague but ever-present unease that's the result of abandoning your principles. Choices will be clearer, and take less time to make.

So, an important part of the process of making our lives less complicated—of uncluttering our lives—is learning to be honest, if we aren't already. That's really essential.

How do you perceive time?

A more tangible step in simplifying your life is actually uncluttering your calendar by limiting or rearranging your obligations. First, think about the meaning of time for you. Is time an enemy or a friend? Do you assume there is too little time? Do you never have time enough to do the things you need to do? Lately our culture has made it seem like this is a desirable state of affairs, and that you're not a success if you don't have a time problem. But being in a constant time crunch is not a desirable state; it's frustrating and mentally constraining and it prevents you from being in the moment.

Unlike money, time is something we all have the same amount of, in the sense that we all have 24 hours in each day. I believe, then, that it's simple: If you do not have enough time, it is because you are not using it wisely. Or you're planning your schedule unrealistically.

For example, if I tell a publisher that I can write an outstanding book in six months, but know in my heart that I need a year, then I am not going to give him the quality book I promised. In addition, I am placing myself under unnecessary stress, and I will be unhappy with the book I turn in. Likewise, If I plan to take part in ten organized activities during a weekend, I'm not going to be able to relax and fully participate in any of them. My mind will always be jumping forward to where I'll have to be in an hour, and how I'm going to get there, and whether I'll have time to change clothes for that next event, and where I can buy what I'm expected to bring. Sound familiar?

Not only do we overschedule our own lives, but today's generation of parents is notorious for overscheduling their children's as well. Many middle-class children—and this goes down to the preschool level—have appointment books as full of obligations as those of CEOs. They have to rush from school to dance class to playoff game to play date, with scarcely a second to take a breath. Where's the time to be a child and just sit and look at the sky? Where's the time to—as I did— bounce around on a chenille-covered bed for the pure, silly joy of it, or to just be with a favorite animal for hours, and "talk" together, in your own ways?

These children didn't take their heavy loads of responsibilities on themselves. Their parents did it for them. People overschedule their own and their children's lives for a number of reasons. The perceived need to keep up with the Joneses is one. Fear of idleness is another. Yet another is the idea that we've absorbed from our advertising culture that if you don't pay for something, it's not of value. That's why people will sign up for an expensive exercise class rather than walk for free in the park, or why parents feel that to spend quality time with their one-year-olds they have to enroll in a structured parent-and-toddler program rather than play peek-a-boo at their leisure, at home.

The Puritan ethic is part of this picture too. Many people have been brought up to believe that if the activity they're engaged in isn't strenuous, demanding, and at least a little bit unpleasant, they're doing something wrong.

With these attitudes, you can easily spend your whole life doing things you don't want to do, things that will never mean much to you or anyone else, except perhaps the people making money from them, and—here's the pitiable part—things you absolutely *don't have to do*. It's scary how much time you can waste. At some point you really ought to ask, "Why am I cluttering my life with all these less than rewarding activities, if I don't have time to relax, or to do what I really enjoy?"

At what point in life do you start including that which is essential to your real nature?

Write down what is essential to your real nature. Are you, deep down, really a writer? An artist? A people-helper? Maybe you love to garden. Or are drawn to cities. Or have always wanted to be an athlete. Or a chef. Maybe you adore dogs. Maybe baseball is truly your passion. Are the things and activities to which you're drawn actually a part of your life right now? Or have you been putting them off for some future time that keeps receding?

Look at the way you live your life. Ask yourself, "Is this what I really want to be doing with my days?" If it is—then great. If it is not, what do you really want to do? If you are working in an institution, for example, would you rather be someplace where you could help people without bureaucratic limitations? Would you rather be someplace where people are not fighting against your efforts to help them? There are places in this world where you will be appreciated for your efforts. Allow yourself to be there.

Do you love your work?

Okay, maybe you can't quit your boring day job to become a renowned musician. But there are ways you can work toward that goal, each day. You can take lessons, you can practice at home, you can take out books from the library on your facet of the art.

Here's the goal I would set for every human being: Do the work you love to do. Follow your passion. Do work that gives your life meaning. Do not just work to make a living. Then you are only working to support a lifestyle cluttered with things that may give you a measure of status but that ultimately rob your life of purpose. Ask yourself, "What purpose do I have?" We all have one. Your purpose in life is what gives your life direction and meaning. Declare what is yours.

Do the "little" things in your life work?

You need to examine every part of your life to assess whether or not it is working for you. This means not just the big issues, like where you work and how you relate to your family and friends, but the little things as well, such as whether you've painted your walls colors that you really like, or whether you've ever gotten around to buying good-quality pots and pans to cook your meals in. It always amazes me how people will go their whole lives with less than optimal living and eating and sleeping arrangements, when they can well afford to have them. It's the "better-keep-the-walls-beige-in-case-we-have-to-sell-the-house" mentality. Whose house is it anyway—the people's who'll be living in it after you're dead?

Make a list of everything in your life you feel is important to you as a physically aware creature. Include small details, the things you don't consider essential but that nevertheless matter to you. For instance, in addition to wall color and kitchenware, think about this: Do you sleep in the kind of bed that you really want to be in, on the kind of sheets that you want next to your body? Do you have a nice, warm comforter? These things can be more important than you think.

Growing up, I spent a lot of time at my aunt's house. My mother worked a lot, and my aunt took care of me and my brothers after school. Whenever we were there, she would insist that we have a nap. She said it would make us healthier. Of course, napping was the last thing we wanted to do. We were full of energy. So we'd go into the room, bounce up and down on the beds, play, sing, and wrestle. Still, I remember the smell in the room, and the feel of being there. The bed had a white chenille bedspread, the kind with little balls all over it. It felt so good and warm that I've spent my whole adult life looking for chenille bed covers, unfashionable though they may be.

Everything about my aunt's house was warm. It was so unlike many of the uncomfortable homes of today. Today, you sit on the furniture and think, "What am I sitting here for? I don't feel good on this. I'm not going to sit on the floor; I'm not going to sit on the window sill; and I can't sit on the radiator because I'll burn myself. But the couch doesn't feel comfortable." You wonder why people ever buy some of the furniture they do.

One reason is that people equate "good" furniture with money and status. They'll say, "What do you think of it? It cost me $3000. I bought it at Bloomingdale's." And remember when we went through that whole phase of putting plastic on everything? The furniture was not only uncomfortable, it made us sweat. Nothing felt like you could nestle into it. The best you could do was melt into it—literally!

I never went in for plastic, or for status furniture. I wanted furniture that was comfortable. I didn't care how it looked, whether it matched or not. I found some big, super-soft couches and sofas. When you sat on them, you felt as if you were sitting on a fluffed-up featherbed. You felt that comfortable. Many times, people would sit on my couch and fall asleep. You should feel totally at ease on a couch.

It's the same with a bed. When you lie on a bed, it shouldn't feel like a board. The idea that a bed should be as hard as a board is a remnant of the Puritan ethic that makes no sense. And forget futons. A lot of people started lying on futons in the 70s because it was the hip thing to do. But sleep on a futon for a night, and you'll see why people go to chiropractors! You get up with aches and bumps and nothing working.

We hate to be honest about what we really want because what we really want is almost never given social approval. Even the color and shape of our clothes is dictated by others. Take a look at your clothes. Do you feel good about what you're wearing? Do you even *feel good* in your clothes, or are they constricting your body, and your breathing? Think of how many times you dressed so as not to stand out. You had to look conservative, you felt, in order to fit in.

Imagine if your choices about what to wear, how to furnish your house, how to spend weekends, and even—or especially— how to spend your life—were dictated not by what you thought others would approve of, but by what *you* really wanted to choose. Life would be so much simpler then because there would be less speculation, guesswork, and self-doubt.

How did you learn what you know?

School

The town I grew up in was less than cosmopolitan. At school, everyone knew everyone else. Some teachers were like fixtures; they had been there for ages. And certain teachers were noteworthy because they taught by the textbook only. Whatever the text said was God's word. They wouldn't deviate from the book. If the textbook was biased, then you learned a biased lesson.

In the South, there were a lot of biases. I always wondered how people could become lawyers, doctors, and judges and still be racist. In the process of becoming more educated, shouldn't they also be able to understand racism and give it up? I found it didn't work that way, and I couldn't figure that out. For the longest time I couldn't figure out how many so-called smart people in our country acted in such irresponsible ways.

I still see highly educated people, like scientists, acting dumb. Many of these Yale- and Harvard-educated people are brilliant in the laboratory. They could regale you with stories related to their field for days. But talk about anything other than what they do and they're no different than anyone else.

People keep themselves very narrowly defined in what they know. Generally, what they know is what they do. What they don't do they don't know about. They don't have balanced lives.

How do we get this way? Well, first, as I've mentioned, there are our teachers. And there is the curriculum, which can be unbalanced for a variety of reasons, including economic ones. When my friend, holistic physician Dr. Marty Feldman was in Yale Medical School and Columbia School of Physicians and Surgeons, he was taught very little about nutrition. Instead, he learned that drugs are a primary source of healing. He was taught that because of the influence of pharmaceutical companies on medical schools. Drug companies are wise enough to endow medical school chairs, which are occupied by people they know will be supporting their particular line of drugs. In the 1950s, there was a mad scramble for pharmaceutical companies to dump tax-exempt money into foundations that would then support these schools. No one was funding research on meditation, biofeedback, alternative lifestyles, behavior modification, or exercise. There was no money in these things.

As a result of these influences, the whole medical field of 650,000 physicians is taught a one-sided approach to healing. They learn methods that often have no science behind them. For example, in the case of breast cancer, taking lymph nodes out of a woman's armpit was standard practice for years, even though there was never any research proving that doing this would increase lifespan. No one considered that the lymphatic system serves the purpose of supporting the body's immune response and aiding detoxification. No one thought that removing a part of this filtration system could result in the person succumbing to the cancer or to something else. So, everything was cut and taken out.

Only now is this beginning to change. But no one has ever apologized to all of the women needlessly mutilated.

When your basic belief system is wrong, then everything you learn and exponentially extend beyond that is also possibly flawed. Wrong knowledge gets passed on.

A woman wrote a book about how to cure cancer with grapes, and everyone thought she was a nut. No one wanted to research what she had said. Well, recently it was proven that grapes help prevent cancer in laboratory animals.

Now you can bet your bottom dollar that they're going to find a chemical within the grape that they can synthesize and make into a patented drug. You won't be told to eat grapes; you'll be told to take that drug. Unfortunately (for you) the drug will be expensive. Grapes aren't. And since the drug will be artificially synthesized, it will have the potential of being toxic. Grapes aren't. But it will be the drug that will be pushed. The paradigm doctors have been taught of "drugs cure, and *only* drugs cure" is going to be pretty hard to overcome.

Family

Another way people learn is by being given information by their families. Some of this is helpful, but much of it can be biased as well.

I met a young Algerian fellow, named Ali. When I had a restaurant, I hired Ali as a chef there. One night I walked into the restaurant unexpectedly, as I had forgotten something. It was late and Ali was on his way out with two shopping bags full of food. I wasn't going to ask about the bags because I had no suspicion. But Ali volunteered, "You caught me." When I asked him what was in the bags he told me he had taken food. Then, when I asked him where he was going with the food he said, "Home." At this point, I was still thinking that he was taking food that we didn't sell or need. Then I learned that Ali had taken whole blocks of cheese. Since the restaurant was not a profit-making venture, the last thing I needed was someone stealing from it.

Ali and I had a long conversation about what happened. I didn't fire him because I learned that he had been taught at home that stealing was necessary. He came from a poor family, and poor families routinely went out each day to steal food.

14

Stealing was almost like a job. Ali believed it was ethical to steal from someone richer. His family had taught him that.

Self-Exploration

Another mode of learning is through self-exploration. This is how we can learn most of our important lessons. Unfortunately, self-exploration is rare. People are reluctant to give credence to their own perceptions. Even if their own experience gives them pleasure, joy, happiness, and excitement, they will not trust their own judgment, if the authorities haven't validated it. Many times I see people experience something real. They love it. But instead of going forward with it, they say, "No, that's not me. I've got to go back here and play it safe. I'd better stick with what's traditional and regular."

"No," I always, in essence, try to say, "you ventured into life. You opened the door, and there you were. You were looking at yourself, beckoning yourself to come forward. You did. You took a step. It was real."

"Uh-uh. I can't rely upon me. I feel too uncomfortable. I'd rather follow the experts. I need my psychologist. My social worker. My 12-step program. I have to go every day and say I'm an addict. They tell me I am. They tell me I've got to live one day at a time and I'm an addict for life. And if I ever try anything again I'll become an addict again. I live with fear, nothing but fear. I'm afraid that if I don't do exactly what I'm supposed to do—come to these meetings, say stupid things, and be with people who smoke and drink coffee, I'm going to be an addict again. Now I'm a passive addict, but I might become an active addict again."

People are so ready to accept others' truths about them.

As a teacher and counselor, I encourage others to go forward.

But if the only time a person does something meaningful is under my guidance, then that person is merely being a follower. The person is merely a parasite to my life process. If I do something, they do something. I stop doing something; they stop doing it. I do it again; they do it. That's not a life. That's being a shadow to someone else.

When people go forward through self-exploration, they don't look for teachers. They accept the inner teacher. The inner teacher resonates as true. Support, yes; indoctrination, no.

Life is just about passages, and all we have are moments of conscious attention in our passages. That's all we have. The wise person self-explores during each passage to get the most out of the journey—and the moment.

Have you ever challenged your formal learning experiences?

Seeing the danger of conformity, I grew up challenging my teachers all the time. I was not impolite, but I challenged them. Growing up in a small town, my teachers were often the same people who had taught my father and my older brother. I had a reputation for saying irreverent or wrong things. So, my challenges weren't taken seriously and I never influenced anybody. But at least I was very honest.

I still don't influence very many people. For years, I thought I was making a difference, not realizing that the people sitting across from me had not committed themselves to real, meaningful change. Desperate when they came to me, these people only showed up after all their experts or doctors said there was nothing more they could do. Still, they were not open to

16

looking at another way of approaching their problems. They came because there was nothing else to do and their families told them that they had to do something so they should go see Gary Null. They would show up at my door as skeptical as ever. No matter what I would suggest for them to do, they would not listen. Oh, they would talk to me, and act like they were considering my words. But then they would go right back to the person who had offered them no help, for instance, a doctor who had told them they had just three months to live.

They would go back and tell the doctor, "Gary Null said I should try ozone therapy."

"That's quackery. Don't do that," the doctor would say.

"Okay, I won't."

To that I would say, "If they're giving you no chance to live, and I give you a suggestion, shouldn't you at least try it?"

Their response: "I don't want to get my doctor angry at me." I've seen this happen hundreds of times.

You should be adopting new ways of approaching problems before the point of desperation. You should be eating right, exercising, and taking chelation therapy before you get a heart attack. That takes self-exploration. But conditioning makes it very hard for most people to change. It prevents them from allowing anything new in. The person is filled with the principles given to them by their mother, father, brother, sister, aunt, uncle, rabbi, priest, and nun. It's all those people inside that someone has to convince before a new experience is allowed in. That's why people have so much guilt, fear and loathing about doing something differently. It's not because of the self that change is not happening; it's because of everyone else's early admonitions and conditioning.

Does curiosity motivate you to learn?

How curious are you? What are you curious about? And what are you willing to do about it? Are you willing to engage your curiosity? Are you willing to transgress boundaries set up by others in order to explore?

Kids are naturally curious in an innocent way. We allow kids to say and do things that we, as adults, do not allow ourselves to do out of fear. What if we were curious about everything and willing to explore completely?

I believe we have the right to explore anything that helps us to discover who we are. I don't believe in drugs or in anything else that is self-destructive. But I do believe in doing anything positive that allows us to grow. Doing this pushes us up against social norms, religious norms, familial norms, political norms, and professional norms.

Most of us adapt to the world's expectations. But we lose ourselves in the process. And the world, in truth, loses something too.

Think of how many surgeons do unnecessary operations knowing they shouldn't do them. What would happen if, out of curiosity, a physician decided to take another route? People would wonder why. Picture the doctor defending his point: "With prostate cancer, it's been shown that whether or not you receive surgery you live equally long. Therefore, I'm not going to do surgery."

"You can't do that, you're a surgeon."

"I know I'm a surgeon, but I'm also a doctor. A doctor is supposed to be a healer. Therefore, I'm going to broaden my approach."

"You can't broaden. You're board-certified!"

Isn't it amazing that the more prestigious you become, the more narrow becomes the scope of what you are supposed to do, say, and be?

Are you willing to look foolish until you get it right?

Have you not done something because you didn't know how to do it? Have you never gone skiing, ice skating, roller blading? What else haven't you done that you would like to do? Have you avoided bicycle riding, dancing, swimming? There are so many great activities you can miss out on if you're afraid you'll look silly trying.

You will, you know. You'll look silly for quite some time until you get these skills right. But so what? Looking silly doing them is so much better than feeling unsatisfied not doing them. Besides, you'll get the skills right sooner or later.

Here's another problem: Perhaps you don't know the "proper" way to respond to certain new things. Have you not seen some interesting foreign language films because you thought you wouldn't know how to react to them? Have you not gone to the ballet or the opera because you might make an "inappropriate" comment about the performance while you were there? And what about saying the "wrong" thing to the waiter at a fancy restaurant? Has that prospect prevented you from ever going to one?

A friend tells me an interesting story about just such a scenario. She had gone to an upscale eatery with several co-workers. It was the kind of New York restaurant where the waiters have their noses in the air and the menu has a lot of expensive dishes with fancy foreign names on it. Everyone chose something to order. But one of her colleagues wanted something that was not on the menu.

"Have you got spaghetti and meatballs?" he asked the waiter.

The waiter was aghast. "Sir, we do not serve spaghetti and meatballs here," were his words, but his meaning was clearly, "Sir, you have said a totally wrong thing, one that marks you as the lowest class idiot that has ever entered this restaurant!"

Many people would have practically sunk under the table after such an exchange, but not this man. "You mean you don't have spaghetti and meatballs here?" he said. "You have all this other stuff on the menu and you don't have spaghetti and meatballs? What kind of a place *is* this?"

My friend had to laugh. Her colleague had just turned the tables on the waiter and made it seem like *he* had said the wrong thing. It was then that she realized that if you have a strong sense of self and know what you want and believe, you're never going to say the wrong thing, because there is no wrong thing to say.

Do you rationalize so you can keep on accepting things as they are?

Think of a time when something wasn't working in your life, and yet you tried to rationalize in order to justify holding on to the situation. The list of common rationalizations is practically endless.

"The pay's good."

"I get medical benefits."

"If I stay another six months, I'll get a bonus."

"You can't beat this rent."

"It's too much trouble to move."

"It's not that bad a relationship. So, we have arguments. Everyone does."

"He doesn't lie all the time."

"He's going through a bad period."

"So, he beats me once in awhile. He has a good side too."

Think of all the times you've made excuses for a situation in order to keep from changing it. How could you improve your life if you stopped rationalizing?

Just accept something or reject it. If it's not right for you, simply let it go.

Do you recognize that your thoughts, feelings, and actions have a physical correlation?

There is cause and effect. You eat something that you shouldn't eat and your body reacts unfavorably. Your body reacts because you have done something to disrupt the body's natural flow. If at the same time you are worried, you create further disharmony. On top of that, expressing yourself negatively creates spiritual disharmony. Now you've caused disharmony on multiple levels. What if we do hundreds of things per day that create a perpetual disharmony? We're creating an environment conducive to disease. Then, we get surprised when we wake up one day and we have a disease.

There's a natural order to life. When you go against it, you always pay a price. The wise person connects with the natural order and does that which is mentally, spiritually, and physically uplifting. Anything that creates an imbalance creates a disharmony that dishonors the consciousness within every cell of our bodies. Following the natural order of life is what gives us our meaning, direction, and purpose in life. People who are just working for a living, people who are just living for a relationship, people who are working to support a standard of living—all are in disharmony. All the excuses and rationalizations in the world will not change that.

At what pace do you function best? Fast? Slow? In between?

Part of the natural order to your own life is your pace. We've all heard about how different people have different rates of internal metabolism; we understand that's why some people have a harder time burning off calories than others. Likewise, when we interact with the external world, each person has a natural speed. Some people naturally function faster than others. That's normal for them, and they'd be frustrated if they had to restrain themselves to others' seemingly snail-like pace. Not that speed is necessarily better than a slow, deliberate course through life. Those who function slowly may consider that the speedsters are missing a lot along the way.

If you can help it, never artificially speed up or slow down to fit into the mold of what society seems to expect. Right now, as we've mentioned, a fast and frenzied pace is in vogue, but not everyone is comfortable with that. In fact, it's making a lot of people sick. So feel what is optimal for you. At what level do you function best? That's the level at which you should maintain your lifestyle. Don't look around for examples from friends, because they are not you. I can do a lot, and it's normal for me. And I can do very little and it would still be all right, but it wouldn't be normal for me. Pace yourself at a comfortable rate. Either speed it up or slow it down so it's perfect for you.

Life is a journey, but just as we don't all take it along the same road, we don't all have to travel at the same speed.

Staying Positive in a Negative World

2

2

Everything in life is about choices. And often we make wrong ones. At the time, we may even suspect that we are making a mistake, but fear, anger, bitterness, and other negative feelings influence our judgment. Only later, when we must face the consequences of our decision, do we truly understand our mistake.

A simple karmic rule states that once something is done, it can never be undone. This is not to suggest that we should avoid making errors. After all, we're only human. What I am suggesting is that we learn from our mistakes and avoid repeating them. In this way we can learn lessons, grow from the experience, and move forward. We can take a negative experience and transform it into a positive one. An example of such a turnaround would be when you get into a conflict with someone—perhaps as a result of something you said but shouldn't have—and then you resolve the conflict by apologizing, ending up with an even stronger relationship than you had in the first place.

This is not all that common an occurrence, unfortunately. How many times in life did you mutter to yourself, after you said or did something, "I shouldn't have said that. I shouldn't have done that. It was stupid. I got my ego in there. I closed a door I shouldn't have closed"? But you didn't go back and apologize.

When is the last time you did apologize about anything? You may not even be able to remember, which is a shame because apologies that come from the heart can clear a lot of negativity. They show that you value your relationship and honesty above ego.

Are you honest?

I grew up in an area of the country where people were honest about things. It was one of the virtues of small-town West Virginia, and of my family in particular. When you grow up in a family where you have to be honest—because if you're not, they call you on it right away—you get used to saying what you feel. That's why now I'll say a thing without thinking about what I say, if I know it's honest. I just say it. And I assume, if there's going to be a consequence, so be it. Anyway, if I started editing everything I said so that no one would be offended by anything I said, I'd never say anything. I'd be a mute. So to me, honesty is not only the best policy—it's the only policy I know how to operate with.

I call honesty a big component of positive energy and of the positive life. Although there are others—like friendliness.

How does positive, friendly energy make you feel?

Recently, while traveling in Florida, it was wonderful to meet strangers who would greet me with, "Hi, how are you?" What a contrast to the way I had been treated in New York! On my way to the airport there, a bicycle messenger had screamed at my cab driver and spit on the window. When my plane landed in Florida, I was approached by a person who said, "It's awfully hot. Let me give you a ride." A total stranger rode me over to the car rental booth for free.

Such friendly behavior proved to be the norm. In a sporting goods store, a salesman spent an hour and a half talking about equipment, even though he knew I wasn't ready to buy anything. In fact, he told me about another store where I could get what I needed at a cheaper price. Such consideration is unheard of in New York. When you walk into a store you're urged to buy what you see now because what you need is about to be discontinued.

Humane treatment continued as I walked into a food store, trying to hurry my orders so as not to anger the five or six people waiting in line behind me. My sense of uneasiness must have been apparent because the clerk said I should slow down, that nobody was in a rush for anything.

Everybody was so nice. Nobody honked their horn the instant the light turned green, as if your delaying to put your foot to the gas for one nanosecond was a mortal affront to those behind you. Nobody in lobbies or elevators avoided eye contact, as if they suspected you of being a recently escaped psychopathic felon who was somehow carrying concealed weapons in your jogging shorts. (In New York, you can encounter the same person on the elevator every morning for three years, and they'll still get nervous and pretend to be reading their mail!) The friendliness in Florida took some getting used to. But after a couple of days there, I felt really good from all the positive energy. And it all comes from people being considerate of other people.

Do you surround yourself with positive people?

We can't all move to friendlier locales. Nor can we ensure that everyone in our lives has a positive attitude. But we can aim for a life filled with those kind of people.

Think of the people around you now, and ask yourself, are we sharing positive energy? Can I trust this person? Do they have my best interests at heart? You'll know when positive energy is there because you'll feel it. Your guard will be down because there will be no need for it. You can be who you naturally are.

Surrounding yourself with positive energy is especially important when you need healing. Unfortunately, lots of relationships are filled with negativity. People express anger and bitterness toward each other, which drains good energy, and creates sickness. How can you possibly heal when that much negativity is being thrown at you? To heal, you need to be surrounded by joy, love, compassion, understanding, and acceptance.

There is, of course, another side to the coin here, which is that *you* want to be a positive influence on those whose lives *you* touch. You don't want to drag others down with defeatist attitudes, or by holding a grudge. I consider holding a grudge

29

to be one of the most emotionally corrosive things you can do, both to yourself and to others.

Let go, already!

If you're a perpetual grudge-holder, there comes a time when you simply have to let go. Train yourself to say, "What am I gaining by carrying on with my negative energy toward someone? What's the purpose of it?" The ability to change that, to forgive, to let go, is crucial to the healing process. It's so healthy to just clear away bad feeling, instead of dragging it around like a dead animal. You begin to smell after awhile if you do that.

It's never healthy when people hold on to negative energy. Have you had this experience in a relationship?—Someone brings something up to you, something that happened a long time ago that you thought was a dead issue? It's over, but all of a sudden they'll say, in essence, "It's not over. We're happy now, for the past nine and a half years of a ten-year relationship, but two months into that relationship, you said this to me. And I've been holding on to this the whole time. It's eating my guts out."

"Oh, really? Why didn't you tell me? What else are you holding?"

"Well, get me angry again, and I'll bring out a whole laundry list!"

Soon the person's got you bringing out your laundry list in retaliation, and you've gotten into a mutually destructive pattern more appropriate to kindergarten than to an adult relationship.

Do you value the simple and authentic?

Positive means simple. When I travel, I spend time talking with people. I'll go out for a run in the morning, and speak with folks I meet. Often I ask them, "Why do you live here?" Many times, I meet people who leave their small town for the big city, only to return. A big metropolis looks glamorous at first, but after awhile, all the crises and turmoil get to them. They get to a point where they decide that they have had enough, that there is something more essential and important in life: the positive simplicity of a more authentic existence.

When you have authenticity in your life, what more do you need? By contrast, when you lead an artificial existence, you never have enough. You can eat lots of junk food and never feel satiated, but all you need is one real food and you're satisfied. It's the same way with junk love, junk relationships, junk jobs, junk friends. They don't fill you up. They may stimulate you, titillate you, excite you, but it's all temporary. In the morning you wake up and realize that it wasn't the experience you had hoped for.

Do you value what you have?

Most people in our society today don't have to work for a living. We work for a certain *standard* of living. Do you realize that people in the poorest strata of American society today, on public assistance, have more than the kings and queens of Europe did 300 years ago? If you get up today, and you're in the poorest town in America, you can still pop something in the oven and immediately have something to eat; they couldn't. You have a toilet; they didn't. You've got running water; they didn't. You've got electricity; they didn't. In the winter, you've got heat; they didn't. They didn't even have kitchens in their castles.

What has happened is that we've forgotten to appreciate and respect what we have. Now we all want something more.

We want a junk life. We want superfluous and valueless toys, food, clothes, gadgets, amusements, spectacles, diversions. Look at our affluent suburbs. Everyone has at least ten times more food, shelter, and clothing than they really need, not to mention countless entertainment options, and they're still complaining.

Are you a complainer, blamer, whiner, moaner?

Complainers never see anything as being right. Perfectionists are the biggest complainers. You never can do anything right enough for them. Nothing is ever good enough. If you feed them a 12-course gourmet meal, and you forget the toothpick at the end, they'll condemn the meal. If you take them on a vacation to paradise, and it rains one day, they'll moan about the rotten weather. The negative always takes precedence.

Recently, I was in a man's house. He was showing me his art collection. When he was halfway through, he started complaining about things he didn't have. I said that I thought he already had an awful lot there. But he insisted that what he had was nothing.

"Don't say it's nothing," I said. "Unless you're living in a Biafran hut, where someone can kill you tonight, and where you're starving to death, you have no right to complain that you have nothing. Don't you think you ought to be a little more positive?"

32

I won't let someone like this complain negatively to me. I just won't listen. I've seen real suffering, and when you've got a perspective like that, you can't help but think that we are a nation of babies.

Now I'm not saying that people living above the African poverty level do not have a right to share their troubles with others, as a way of seeking support, help, and suggestions for positive change. I don't believe people have to be stoic or secretive about their problems, and it's certainly okay to vent your emotions when you're feeling frustrated, angry, or scared. But vent once. Vent twice. Don't keep venting, and venting, and venting, making dissatisfaction a way of life. Chronic complainers have absolutely no intention of making any positive changes; you could hand them a foolproof plan for improving their life on a silver platter, and they still wouldn't take it.

When you hear someone like this begin to complain, or to blame someone or something, stop them before they get going. Let them know that you don't want them sharing that negative energy with you.

Stop the moaners too. Stop them, and say, "Hold on. Is there something else you can do besides moan?" When you tell someone they're moaning, they'll stop. If they start again, remind them. Say to them, "Don't share this with me. You can moan to those who want to hear it, but I don't. I'm in my sanctuary. If you want to come into my house, into my heart, and into my mind, respect who I am. Don't dump your emotional garbage on me. It dishonors me."

Also recognize when you do it to yourself.

Do you blame the world when you feel bad, angry, or helpless?

People blame the world for how they feel all the time. What if you were to stop blaming others for how you feel? What if you changed how you felt, instead?

Before reacting to your feelings, find a quiet place, and take a moment to sit down and ask yourself if you can make yourself feel any different. For example, if someone says something about you that you don't like, and that's not true, instead of getting angry, you could have an inner dialogue that goes something like this: "It's just some words. That's all it is. I'm more than some words. And I'm certainly more than what someone thinks of me. It's what I think of me that counts. If everyone thinks I'm bad, and I know that I'm good, I have to accept that I'm good. I'm not going to accept what other people assume that I am. Therefore, I'm not going to allow myself to be angry with anyone or with myself."

We can change the way we deal with something that's thrown at us. We don't have to become victimized by it.

Do you express who you really are?

When we are in touch with who we really are, we are positive and light because we let the spiritual part of ourselves emerge. This is the part of us that wants to proclaim itself, to come out and speak. Sometimes it's easy to get in touch with this part of our nature because we've had good parents and friends, and a supportive environment.

At the other extreme, we may be completely out of touch with who we really are. Everything we do is influenced by the

34

conditioned mind. We look for the rewards we can gain, and aren't motivated by the sheer joy of doing something. This often stems from being raised in a family where we weren't accepted for who we really were. Perhaps our parents only accepted us if we brought home a perfect report card: "If you don't get an A, you're grounded." We were made to feel that something we do is the key to acceptance and love. Getting a B or worse made us no longer lovable. Thus we learned to believe that we're not a good person for who we naturally are. That becomes our reality, and it can manifest all through life in self-doubt, low self-esteem, and the inability to try anything where we risk not succeeding.

Show me a child who was given unconditional love, and I'll show you a child who is not afraid to do anything because they know they'll be accepted, no matter how many times they fail at something. Failure is not equated with a character fault. It's merely a learning experience. These fortunate children are allowed to grow through their mistakes.

Is how you spend your time reflective of who you are?

Being in or out of touch with who we are is reflected in the work we do. Many people work hard, but do so because they are addicted to their work, meaning they use work as a way to escape from themselves. Others work hard but do so for the love of it. Picasso slept in front of his paintings because he loved his work. To him, work was not an addiction, but a passion.

Take a moment to assess how you spend your time. Pull back from your daily routine and really look at it to see if it expresses who you are. Is your day so filled with appointments that you never have quality time for yourself and others? Is your work fulfilling in itself? Does it allow you to express a part of yourself? Or is it just a job? What things do you really love to do? Are you doing them?

Are you trustworthy?

I counsel a lot of well-known people. And I can't tell you how many times journalists have asked me about different celebrities. But I would never talk about them. I never even keep records because I don't want information getting into the wrong hands.

You never see successful people betraying anyone. Positive, happy, balanced people don't need to live through someone else's pain and suffering.

Are you a taker without being a giver?

I have a daily radio program on a noncommercial radio station that depends on audience support for its existence. Many of my listeners tune in every day, and have done so for years. From the show, they get valuable information, not just from me but from a variety of top-rate sources on health, nutrition, and more. But only five percent of my radio audience supports WBAI. Now what does that tell you? It tells me that most people are selfish. Who, but an absolutely negative person, would take so much positive, life-enhancing, even life-saving information and never give back anything in return? It seems awfully selfish to me.

When one of my unsupportive listeners says they're not

selfish, I ask him or her, "How much do you have to get before you can give?" Suddenly, they're challenged. "What do you mean by that?" they ask. "Well," I reply, "if someone gives you 1000 hours of knowledge for free, how much is that worth? What would you pay for that if you went to college? Wouldn't you think that a small pledge to the station might be appropriate in return?"

When a person is unwilling to give, and only takes, it shows something about their character. I'm willing to bet that the WBAI "takers" deal with everyone similarly. I believe they take advantage of everyone, whenever they can.

Are you flexible enough to go with the flow? Or are you stuck with rigid ideas, patterns, and images?

Nearly 25 million Americans have lost their jobs in the past 20 years. Now, many people who are being laid off are not minimum-wage earners. They're people who were coming home with $75,000, $100,000, and $200,000 a year.

Do you know what some of these people don't do? They don't make any changes. They're afraid to change their lifestyle because they're afraid it will change their image, and their image is more important than anything else. So they keep holding on to their previous standard of living. In the process they go through their savings, cash in their insurance policies, sell their furnishings, and so on, until all the money is gone. Then they blame the world for not giving them another job like the one they left. Their egos won't let them change.

What does it say when someone wants to have what they had, and is not willing to transform any part of their life? It means they're rigid and stuck. These affluent people who have lost their jobs could be looking upon their circumstance as an opportunity—to try out new skills, to take stock of their lives, to develop parts of themselves that were previously dormant. I'm not trying to sugarcoat their situation, but they could be using it as an opportunity for learning.

One of the things they could be learning is that *you* don't change because something is lost. The essential *you* is the same after the loss as before. It's just that now you can't hide behind your high-status job and your salary.

When making changes, do you surround yourself with positive people?

At no time is it more important to have positive people around you than when you are making changes in your life. So you might want to reconsider who you have in your life at those times. I only want positive people in mine, people who believe very much in what they're doing. Those are the ones who are going to believe in what *I'm* doing.

Negative people can drain you. They will try to thwart your plans before you begin acting on them. Fortunately, there are enough positive people in this world to make being around negative ones unnecessary.

Down at my ranch, I advise people to separate from others who are negative. People are there to heal, to contemplate new directions, and they need quiet, peaceful time. There will usually be a small group of negative people who criticize everything going on. I have to send people home because of that. Often they don't understand why they were sent home. They don't see it because being negative is such a part of them.

Do you pay more attention to the prophets of doom or the prophets of happiness?

Doom usually gets the attention, while happiness is usually ignored. Impending doom creates the need for urgency, and it gives negative people something to blame for their lives not working. Each day is the same for negative people. There's never anything new and bright to look forward to.

Have you ever noticed how negative people get together and share negative energy? And it strengthens them. They can go on forever. They don't get tired.

"Give it a break! Give it up for a moment!"

"No, we're happy, we're trashing, we're gossiping. Leave the room; we'll gossip about you."

Positive people are too busy living meaningful lives to talk about others. They're too excited about living each moment. Each day is another day to live, another experience, another adventure.

What happens when you anticipate the worst-case scenario?

When you believe something will happen, it probably will. By anticipating the worst-case scenario, you are focusing your thoughts in a negative direction. Since action and emotions follow thought, your expectations have a good chance of being manifested.

People think negatively because on some level it benefits them. They may not like the consequences of their thoughts, but it helps them to identify who they think they are.

Do you sabotage yourself by creating unachievable expectations?

Think of the things that you want to achieve. How realistic are they? When you don't achieve what you set out to do, do you blame everyone else for your not having accomplished your goals? Many people set expectations far in excess of what they need. There is a big gray area between what they need and what they try to achieve.

Set realistic expectations. Accept that you are capable of being more than you currently are. But don't make what you want impossible to attain.

Ask for what you want or need.

Are there things you need, but don't ask for? Do you feel undeserving or that you will not get them? I suggest that you ask for what you need. Otherwise, you will continue to live without your essential wants and needs being met.

Are you the epicenter of your own experience, or do you seek validation from friends and family?

When you experience something, do you look at it, realize what it is, and then let it go? Or do you immediately get on the phone and talk to people about it? Most people seek validation from someone else. Most people don't even know what they've experienced. They can't even trust their experience.

Imagine what it would be like if we didn't have to have anyone else validate our experience? We could do it ourselves. Do you realize how much you could let go of in a hurry? Do you realize how much time you would have that you would otherwise be wasting with endless talking that never gets you anywhere?

Describe your negative self-talk, and you'll be able to start the process of change.

Negative patterns of behavior repeat themselves all day long. Let's say there's something that you cannot handle, or there's something not happening that you wish would happen, or there is a situation in your life that you're not able to be in control of and you wish you were—if you're negative you're going to talk out the problem all day long. But you will always be defeatist about it. When people feel overwhelmed, used, hurt, unable to control the outcome of events, or betrayed, they tend to look at themselves as victims.

What would happen if, instead of all this negative self-talk, you started positive self-talk, and stopped yourself every time you started in with the negative? Say, "Hold on. This is going nowhere. I'm not going to feel good after this. What can I do in place of the negative?"

That's how the process of change begins. First, identify when you're engaged in negative self-talk. Second, don't let the negative go beyond you. Don't allow the negative self-talk to generate the emotion that causes the action. Then you get the reaction that you don't like the consequences of. Stemming this negative pattern keeps you from unnecessary arguments, unnecessary accusations, unnecessary condemning, unnecessary blaming, unnecessary complaining, and allows you then to be at the epicenter of your life.

Third, replace the negative with the positive. Look at the

positive options for solving your problem or improving your situation. Select the one or several that seem the best. And then start implementing them, not in a panicked, desperate way, but with resolve and balance.

Happy people are balanced.

Look at people who are the happiest. They're always balanced in their life. There are never excesses there. There's never an extreme. There's always a positive energy, but it's often a subtle energy.

The negative, by contrast, is spastic, volatile, and highly excitable. It exaggerates, and draws attention to itself. It's insecure.

Have you ever noticed the following? When someone attains a success they don't deserve, they don't know how to deal with it. They almost always promote their success, as if they have to prove that they deserve it. They're insecure about what they have because they know they can lose it at any time, and often they do.

When people are legitimately happy and successful, they're understated; they're quieter. You don't see them parading their success around. They don't have to because what they have is well-deserved; it's theirs and no one can take it away from them.

Happiness isn't a state; it's a skill.

Advertising and other parts of popular culture have led us to believe that happiness is a state you achieve after you've managed to accumulate the right set of possessions. Nothing could be further from the truth.

Happiness isn't a state; it's a skill. It's the skill of knowing how to take what life throws your way and make the most of it. It's the skill of intuiting what you should be doing during your time on the planet, and then of making choices so that you can actually be doing it.

Some of those choices may not be popular ones. And ironically, having the "right" set of possessions may get in the way of your making them. But they're your choices, your chances at happiness. Make them boldly, and your world will be transformed.

3
Creating Content-ment

3

Where can happiness be found? It's an age-old question, answered differently in different cultures. In America, people tend to look for something outside of themselves to bring them happiness. They spend a lot of time and energy to get something to make them feel better inwardly. They strive for a better job, for instance, or a bigger house, or a larger family. People are always saying, "If only I had more money, I wouldn't have all of these problems." It's assumed that the lack of money or things is the cause of their inner discord.

This idea is contrary to experience. When most people are first dating, for example, they generally don't have a lot of money. Still, they're happy and excited. They've got each other, they've got passion, and they've got boundless energy and joy.

Later on, they often have everything that money can buy—but they've lost that happiness. Eventually, they wake up and experience a crisis. Suddenly they're 30 or 40 or 50, and they have many things, but no happiness. Something is wrong inside. They have feelings of irritation, emptiness, and loneliness. Their lives are not working.

Many people react by doing what they've always done. They

get new and more possessions, such as fancier cars and computers. Some people replace the people in their lives. They find a new boyfriend, girlfriend, husband, or wife. Others lose themselves in their work. Men, in particular, tend to become overly responsible and work longer hours than necessary. Such actions, though, are merely momentary distractions that never address the root cause of the problem.

It's difficult for us in the U.S. to comprehend people of other cultures who choose not to chase these illusory dreams. But such an attitude exists in many cultures, such as in India or Tibet, where people commonly lead happy lives without needing to have things. And even in countries that are closer to us, culturally, than India, there are differences in attitude. England comes to mind. Personal possessions there are fewer, smaller, and older than in the U.S. Homes and other buildings are generally smaller and older too. But these differences are in no way negatives, and the English people don't seem any the worse for them.

Visiting London, you have to downsize your expectations if your eyes are focused to an American's typical perspective. It took me a little while to do that, when I was there. For instance, I'll never forget the time I couldn't find the Palladium. The Palladium is a world-famous London concert hall, sort of like New York's Radio City or Carnegie Hall. I'd consulted a map, so I knew the location of this attraction. But walking up and down the street, I couldn't find the place. It was nowhere to be seen. Concluding that the map was wrong, I was about to move on, but I figured I'd consult a cab driver first.

"It's right there," he said, pointing to a spot just behind me. And sure enough, there it was. I'd overlooked it because the renowned Palladium was—well—little. We have Gap stores larger than this.

My experience with theater in London was similar. As on Broadway, tickets for plays were offered at various prices, depending upon the section of the theater you sat in. Figuring that, as on Broadway, if you got the cheapest ticket you'd need binoculars to see the play, I opted for a costlier seat. But at showtime I discovered that that wasn't necessary. The theater was tiny! Compared to New York theaters, there were a ridiculously small number of rows in each section, and I could have had an intimate theater experience from any seat in the house.

In fact, that was a big part of the appeal of England— everything was intimate and personal because it was small in scale. Monuments, castles, restaurants, and inns were practically miniature by American standards, but there was a charm and personalness in that that made visiting them a delightful experience. There was also a factor of age that added to the charm. It's not unusual for an English inn to be several hundred years old, and to still be served by its original wood plank floors and stone walls. Homes too, are hundreds of years old; there's nothing out of the ordinary for an English family to be living in a centuries-old house that here would have landmark plaques nailed up all over it and be featured in magazines. Of course, here, most such buildings have been razed long ago, as have many of their replacements. We're always looking for something new.

I talk to people when I travel because I like to get a sense of how people live, day-to-day. I found out that in England prices for necessities are similar to what they are here, for a whole range of things, like houses and cars and haircuts and food.

But the English, on average, earn less than people here do—20 to 50 percent less. How do they manage, especially when gas, food, rent, clothes, and entertainment are about the same cost?

Their expectations are different. The English do it by having realistic standards for what one should possess, by valuing what they do possess, and by taking care of their assets.

And not just of their own personal assets, by the way, but of their communities'. For instance, London's Hyde Park, comparable to New York's Central Park but a mile smaller, was a sparkling showpiece compared to it—graffiti-less, immaculate, and with lawn chairs left out and left standing. Another asset of the English is their pretty countryside. It's not spectacular in the sense of a Yosemite National Park, but you can see that they value their landscape in the way they maintain footpaths throughout it. You can walk through that whole country.

On a personal level, the English are not into waste. They buy clothes with an eye to quality and years of use. "I don't have a thing to wear!" people here wail, even when they've got wardrobes stuffed with clothes. But consider an English closet. It's not unusual for a husband and wife to share one small one. That's all they need. Each member of the couple may have only one work outfit, one formal outfit, and one casual one. Their footwear collection would be along those lines too.

Some English austerity is a proud holdover from the Spartan lifestyle that kept the country going during World War Two. Some of it just stems from necessity. I don't mean to glamorize the English, because no people have a corner on virtue. But I do understand the pull of England and other "quaint" countries, for Americans. I felt that pull myself. It's not just an "Isn't that cute?" thing. It's a sense that life's more intimate and nurturing, more manageable in scale. It's Main Street versus a mega-mall; it's the corner store versus Wal-Mart; it's a cozy old house with a little garden versus a colossus of a residence with a killer lawn. For many people it's a reconnection to what had existed at one time, perhaps in their own childhoods.

Do the different values of the English mean that they're happier than we are? I wouldn't presume to say for sure. Although I'd guess yes. At any rate, they didn't seem *less* happy, even though they generally had less than we do in terms of possessions, and what they had was smaller. Touring that country, I couldn't help but think about whether we Americans are too busy trying to create contentment the wrong way—with things. I thought about how the English didn't seem to feel that they had to *have* enough in order to *be* enough. There wasn't this constant acquisition and discarding of things, including clothes, houses, and even values, for that matter. Rather, there seemed to be a respect for what you already had, in its purity. There was a pervading sense that some things were not meant to be changed, but rather nurtured and enjoyed, for a long long time.

Do you try to possess things as if you can find your happiness within them?

In our culture people don't usually want things for survival reasons. Rather, they think that things will make them feel good. So they work to maintain or elevate their standard of living. This makes them feel more accepted, and they use this acceptance as a basis for self-esteem. They need someone else's acknowledgment to make them feel okay. And that's the way it has to be if you carry around a projection of who you should be based on the expectations of parents, friends, schoolteachers from the past, or even commercial advertisements.

Much of this process is subconscious. People live like robots, accumulating lots of material possessions, achievements, and responsibilities. But if they're not doing it for themselves, sooner or later they may begin to realize that they have no real life. They're living in a dream.

There comes a time when you need to wake up. You've got to awaken and ask yourself, "Who am I?" Because until you look within, you won't have the opportunity for lasting happiness and fulfillment.

In what do you find pleasure and beauty? And how often do you allow yourself these moments?

Everyone finds beauty in waterfalls, sunsets, and other natural wonders. How often do you give yourself time for these things? If you are like most people, the answer is once in awhile. You might watch the sunset while on vacation. But there is a sunset every night.

If you take the beauty and pleasure out of life, you're left with a functional existence. You pay the rent, the mortgage, the car payments. You hope one day to become rich and powerful enough to enjoy your leisure. In reality, though, people busy making money often become busier than ever once they've made it. I know people who could go anywhere but choose to remain in their Wall Street offices and make more money.

At what point do they have enough to feel that they can enjoy the beauty and pleasure of life? Generally, they never do, unless they have a stroke or some other life-threatening illness.

At that point, they may suddenly realize the importance of beauty and pleasure. I'm suggesting we reprioritize our lives so that what is most important comes first.

What is the message of a crisis?

We all experience crises. A loved one dies, we lose a job, or we have to move. During these times, it's important to ask ourselves the following questions: "What's the message here?" "What can I learn from this experience?" The Chinese interpret a crisis as an opportunity as well as a danger. We must appreciate the occasion for what it can teach us, as well as dealing with the situations as they arise.

Many times a crisis can be avoided by attuning ourselves to our inner needs and taking action before an emergency arises. An example of this can be seen in the person who eats healthfully and meditates, thereby avoiding an otherwise imminent heart attack. The opposite situation can be seen in the experience of a friend of mine who had a stroke after refusing to pay attention to the warning signs.

I had attempted to convince this friend to go to my ranch to detoxify his system and to meditate on his life. He refused to listen. In his mind, everything else was more important than health.

As I had predicted, he had a stroke. Now he's in bad shape—bedridden and in fact totally immobile—and has no choice but to slow down and think about taking care of himself. He has to put his life into perspective and examine what is really important to him. It's a sad situation, but the point is, he himself created this crisis state by ignoring the warning signs that were leading up to it. By attending to his real needs beforehand, he could have prevented the crisis from occurring.

Sometimes a crisis forces us to speed up and take immediate action for change. I lecture a lot in Santa Fe and Albuquerque, where the audience is comprised largely of former New Yorkers. These people generally don't live in the $800,000 homes in the hills but choose to live moderately in an environment that sustains them. Two people who attend my lectures demonstrate how difficult but necessary this transition sometimes is.

This couple comes from a burnt-out neighborhood in Brooklyn where drugs, street gangs, and crime are rampant. They found it difficult to leave the neighborhood they had known their whole lives, but the seriousness of the situation finally forced them to do so. By the time they decided to leave New York, the police weren't able to do enough to stop crime. The highlight, or rather, nadir, of their crisis occurred after the woman was beaten up in the school where she taught.

This event propelled them to ask themselves, "Is there any place in this world that we can call home? Is there a place where we can work and enjoy life without feeling that we're in a combat zone? Is there a place where people will appreciate the lessons we're trying to share?"

With these questions in mind, they took action to change their situation. They bought a trailer and travelled around the United States. They found the answers they were looking for in Albuquerque, where they have since settled down.

We can do the same if we question the situation surrounding our crisis and search for the answers, trusting that a solution is there. Note: Sometimes the solution involves being unpredictable and doing something that no one expects from us. Often it involves changing the way we've been living up to this point. But it's imperative at these times that we pay attention to our own inner needs because only then can we regain homeostasis, or balance.

When we feel discomfort, what is our first response?

We all experience discomfort. We feel it when we take the kids out of one school and put them into another, when we start a new job, or when we end a relationship. Most of us try to escape this feeling. We overeat, drink, go for a drive, panic, or withdraw.

What if, instead of avoiding the experience, we take the opposite approach and immerse ourselves in it? We can take this attitude: "I don't feel good right now, but I'm going to learn something from what is happening." Immersing ourselves in what we're feeling, no matter how uncomfortable, and learning from it, is the only way we can ultimately resolve our problems. Otherwise, we repeat the experience over and over.

One situation that exemplifies this point is in athletics. I see lots of people jogging and racewalking in the park. Yet many of them never show much real physical improvement. They don't lose a whole lot of extra weight. This is because they're only working at their comfort level. When they feel discomfort, they hold themselves back from going any further. They don't push through their discomfort. They view any uneasiness as a barrier to further change. The mind acknowledges these limits and says, "I can't go any further."

If we never allow ourselves to experience feelings of discomfort, we never learn, change, or grow. We begin to feel helpless.

If we face our feelings of discomfort, on the other hand, we learn, we grow, we pick ourselves up, and we forgive ourselves. We get through every crisis and create a new sense of exhilaration in our life.

How do we stop ourselves from being happy?

While we don't consciously try to subvert our own happiness, there are habitual attitudes we sometimes adopt that have the same effect.

Needing to have others validate us

I went back to school only to later realize that I needn't have done so. I did it because I was trying to conform to the expectations of society, which acknowledges academic credentials as measures of your intellectual worth.

I now realize that when people reject you, often nothing in the world that you do will change their opinion of you. For instance, when people spurn others because of their culture, color, gender, or beliefs, there is, many times, nothing that can be done to change their attitude, because their minds are closed—and they long ago threw away the key.

This was an important lesson for me to have learned. I now know that we needn't go through life achieving things to prove to others that we're okay.

Fear of loss

Frequently, we hold on to things we don't need because they are associated with an image we have of ourselves. The things are merely part of a picture we've created to conform to the expectations of others.

55

When we're no longer afraid of losing what we have, we are free. We're no longer concerned about someone else's perception because we know who we are.

Fear of failure

Because many of us are preoccupied with how others see us, we can't be comfortable with ourselves unless we feel perfect. But think of all our bad hair days, how many times a day our breath smells, all the times we look in the mirror and don't like the way we look. Think of how many times we do something that doesn't turn out exactly right. If we can't be comfortable with ourselves during all these times, we're spending an awful lot of our lives in a state of unease.

We shouldn't expect ourselves to be perfect. People in sports achieve proficiency only with practice. Actors who seem so flawless on the movie screen do so only after many rehearsals. Perfection is an illusion. When you see Frank Sinatra singing, Nancy Kerrigan skating, or Joe Namath throwing a football, there are moments when it all seems so effortless. In reality, there was a great deal of trial and error involved in getting to that point. That's what we don't see. We don't see the outtakes, we don't see the mistakes or the confusion, just the final performance.

We judge ourselves too harshly, acting as if everything we say and do were the final product. We need to focus on being honest about who we are rather than worry about being right all the time. Don't look at your life as a performance.

Loss of spontaneity

When we are not in control of our life, but living according to the expectations of others, we lose our spontaneity. Why is spontaneity so important? It allows us to be who we are and to be in the moment. It allows us to feel. Children are always spontaneous. That's why they're honest and unpredictable; we never quite know what they're going to do or say. It's also why they're happy.

Children know how to live in the moment, which is something we often forget as adults. Imagine if we had to pay for each day. How differently we would live! But life's free and we generally take it for granted. Then one day we wake up and realize it's almost over, and that we've wasted a lot of it. If we lived in the moment, we would never feel our time was wasted.

Being spontaneous allows us to live life to the fullest. People ask me how I'm able to write several books, produce a number of full-length documentaries, go to movies and plays each week, maintain meaningful friendships, spend connected time with my family, and travel extensively—all within a year. I can do so because I never waste a moment. Also, I'm fully present in each moment. When I'm physically present, I'm emotionally present as well. I listen to the person I'm with, not just to myself.

The constant desire for more

I grew up around older people. I'll never forget one woman, Hattie, who lived on my corner. She was always happy and singing in her backyard. Hattie would make me sassafras tea and tell me stories.

I saw her again after college, when I was in my early twenties. I asked, "Hattie, why have you always been so happy?" She said, "Whatever I have, I consider a gift, and I cherish every gift I've been given."

Hattie wasn't talking about the things that money can buy.

She didn't have too many of those. But she enjoyed the flowers, the sun, reading, and what she could do. She had shelves filled with books, all of which she read. Hattie would say, "I've got eyes. Why do I need to watch television when I can learn from the richness of these literary minds?" Television was too passive for her. "I don't want to just be entertained," she would say. "I want to engage my mind." The most beautiful garden on the entire block belonged to Hattie. Everybody admired it.

Other people in my home town could have had beautiful gardens too, but they didn't feel it was important. They could have read books, but they didn't find the time. They could have enjoyed the day, but they didn't make the time. They always thought that something else was more important than being in the moment. They would often complain about what they didn't have. "If only I had this I would be happy," they would say, or "I wouldn't have ulcers if I had this." The truth was that people like Hattie, who didn't have very many things, but who knew how to appreciate life, were the ones without the ulcers and with the greatest happiness.

Trying to recreate enjoyable moments

Sometimes we do understand that it's how we spend our time—not what we have—that can make us happy. But we fall into this particular trap: We try to recreate enjoyable moments from the past. Think of how much of our life is based upon repetition. We tend to want to have the same fun in the same way. We think that just because something happened once it can happen a hundred times. In actuality, though, we limit our lives by trying to regrasp something that we enjoyed. We can't have a moment unless we're spontaneous and we let it be what it is. We should never try to recreate it; it can't be recreated.

Nothing can ever be the same again. It can be different—even better—but it can't be the same.

Inability to appreciate what we have

Often we appreciate something only once we no longer have it. The friend I talked about earlier who is laying helplessly in bed now appreciates what his legs and arms could do. I'm sure he'd give anything in the world to have that ability back now.

Think of people whom we've had in our lives whom we never made an effort to spend quality time with, people who have since died. If only they could come back for a short time, how different we would be. Suddenly, we'd know that we had a period of time to share what was meaningful.

Why wait until we don't have something any longer? Why not appreciate what we have today? Take an inventory of what you have in the way of friends, family, and assets, that you can enjoy. Your list may not be as long, materially, as that of a Trump or a Rockefeller, but on the other hand, your inventory will contain people, opportunities, and assets that are unique to you and so truly priceless that you wouldn't trade them with anyone in the world, for anything.

When you take inventory this way, you may realize how much you've learned and experienced in your life. Look at what you've done that has given you happiness. Start to make a list in your diary of the things that have given you great joy in your life. You will begin to see that good feelings stem from you, and that you can renew that joy.

Working Toward Self-Sufficiency

4

4

Have you ever spent time in the Italian countryside?

Picture an evergreen-sprinkled hill. Eight to fifteen stone and wood houses are nestled on the side of this hill, flanked by low stone walls and hand-tilled fields beyond. In fact, every house, fence, and field in this village has to be hand-built or tended because this is not the kind of hill that you can get machinery on.

During a recent visit to the Italian countryside, I would run 10 to 20 miles daily, going from one tiny village like this to another and enjoying the picturesqueness of it all. But what I really marveled at was how much the people in these areas had done with their own hands, and were doing. For instance, in the early morning hours, when I ran, they'd be baking. And I'd see chickens, sheep, and goats, suppliers of eggs, wool, and milk for the villagers. I'd see horses, helpers with the farm labor. I did get to meet many people in the countryside—there aren't more hospitable people anywhere—so I got to enter homes and see how people lived and the extent of their self-sufficiency. It was impressive.

These people could just about do it all! They were their own builders, masons, plumbers, and carpenters. They were their own farmers and gardeners and vintners too—in addition to its own garden, each house had its own vineyard and pressed its own grapes for wine. Plus they had herb gardens and grew an astonishing number of herbs that they used medicinally, as well is in cooking. Some of their home apothecaries would be unmatchable in variety by any store here. So you could say that, in many cases, they were their own doctors and pharmacists too.

With all these things to do, basically to maintain their lives, the people in these Italian villages were busy. I noticed, though, that there was a pacing to their busyness; there was no frenetic quality to it but rather a constancy, interrupted by needed relaxation periods. The key to their scheduling success: They didn't waste time on what I call make-work stress. They stuck to essentials.

Some people in the U.S. are returning, or making a first-time transition, to this kind of simpler, more self-sufficient life. They're moving out to the Santa Fe, or Tucson, or Salt Lake areas, and setting up a back-to-basics type of existence. Interestingly, this is happening in Italy as well. I was told that many Italians who'd grown up in small villages, and were now in their 40s and 50s, were making a move back to rural areas after having enjoyed successful careers in the cities. It seems that the appeal of the self-sufficient life is universal.

I've always valued the concept of self-sufficiency myself. But when I think of this ideal I broaden the concept, because I see self-sufficiency not just as a matter of whether you can bake your own bread or build your own furniture, although these are wonderful skills to have. The way I see it, being self-sufficient also involves mental and emotional components. So it's a matter of whether you can form your own opinions and plans, and stick with them. It's a matter of directing your own life and supporting yourself emotionally, even during those times when no one else is, as they say, "there for you."

Self-sufficiency in the physical and emotional areas may be related; that is, to the extent that you're self-sufficient physically, you have more chance of being emotionally balanced. Of course that doesn't mean that we who live in the cities should all pack up and move to farms so that we can grow our own food. But perhaps there are things that we could be doing for ourselves that we aren't. Examples: baking our own bread, growing our own herbs in kitchen flowerpots, entertaining ourselves with conversation rather than electronically, taking charge of our own health, becoming involved in our local governments or school systems, so that we can affect what happens in our communities.

Being self-sufficient is not an easy thing. It's not a total thing either—nor should it be. But I do see it as a valuable principle and a goal worth working toward. That's why I believe we should all periodically examine our lives to take stock of our own strengths. We should look at ways to develop them too.

Have you ever correctly assessed your own potential? Or are you habitually selling yourself short?

People can generally achieve a lot more on their own than they think they can. I believe you can achieve independence, confidence, self-control, and self-esteem, taking responsibility that's appropriate for yourself and, where necessary, for others. You can achieve just about anything. Of course if you feel that you are limited in what you can achieve on your own, then to the degree that you believe you can't do something, you absolutely will not try. You will stop yourself. You will gridlock and block. Then what you want won't happen, because you won't believe that you can do it. You'll blame not having the right teacher, the right parents, or the right financier.

Being self-sufficient requires effort, and it does not come naturally to everyone. I had a clear example of that a few years ago when I took some people from New York who wanted to learn about alternative lifestyles to my ranch. Dr. Martin Feldman and I started a project. We set aside ten acres and offered people half of everything that they grew. We bought them seeds, books, and machinery. We spent about $30,000 on this project. Five New Yorkers went down there with varying backgrounds. We told them that the plan of action was to remain positive, to read and to learn, and to garden, grow, and market. They loved the idea.

Within two months, the New Yorkers had squandered everything. Weeds were growing. Nothing had been planted. They were into interpersonal politics and relationships to the exclusion of doing anything productive. In fact, they were doing nothing but staying up all night and watching television. They were running up $500 a week bills for organic produce that they were buying in a store to eat. I finally had to send them on their way because they were unappreciative of the opportunity they had been given.

I then brought in a Mexican family, and within three weeks everything got done. The gardens were perfectly manicured and food was growing. It was amazing; they had that place blooming. In one of my conversations with the father, he said, "We come from a very poor area in Mexico where we have to do everything for ourselves. We don't work fast but we work consistently. We think about what has to be done and then use all of our resources to do it. If you ever watch Mexicans work, you will notice that we work at a constant pace and always get the job done. We don't work fast and then burn out." He was absolutely correct, and his words were actually a great capsule description of how to master the art of self-sufficiency. By the way, the slow and steady work pace he described was the same one I later observed in those Italian villages.

Here in urban America we have services to do everything for us. Yes, this is convenient and time-saving, and can help us concentrate on our careers. But the down side of having all these services is that it can lead us to feel helpless in many areas of life, so that in the face of any problem, we focus only on the problem. We step away and say, "I can't do anything."

I hired a friend of mine a while back, someone who had run a big, successful advertising agency. At first I thought that his having been an executive would be a plus. Soon, though, I noticed that week in and week out he would only focus on the problems. He would stop working and nothing would get done. Finally, I asked him if it had ever occurred to him to be positive and to look for solutions. It seemed that the experience of running an agency had gotten him so used to looking at the negative and to blaming others or having others do things for him that he was incapable of coping with problems on his own. All he could do was delegate responsibility to other people.

In our society you see too many people living like that. Then you see why, from a certain perspective, it's good that American corporations are shaking out all that middle management. These are often the people who have lost the art of doing anything for themselves. If you want to get something done, give it to someone who is used to doing things for himself—especially someone who's had to for reasons of survival.

What don't you need or want from others?

I can do it myself, thank you.

This is a phrase I like to keep in mind because I think we generally take too much from others, sometimes in the guise of help. But to give a new spin to an old phrase, with help like this, who needs hindrance? Sometimes you're better off going it alone.

Let's look at a few examples of what you don't need or want from others. This is important in helping you to identify what not to allow into your life. It can help you break the pattern of letting something unhealthy into your life over and over again. Stop accepting what you don't want and don't need by being honest and saying, *This is something I don't want and don't need. Thank you but no. I'd rather do it myself.*

Dishonesty

No one should live with dishonesty. Take a survey of all the places in your life where dishonesty is part of the relationship. Look at your interactions with co-workers, friends, and family. Do you engage in dishonest relationships, or are you able to say, "This is no good. I don't want this"? Once you assert what you won't accept from others, you'll stop dishonesty from entering your life.

I only maintain honest relationships. Once people dishonor me in some way, they are out of my life forever. I don't care what we've shared in the past. A person has to reaffirm today, and people who continue to work with me year in and year out understand that. Those who think that just because they've been with me for a month or two they can drift into not being on time, or not paying attention to the quality of their work because they've been accepted, are wrong. Those people are out. I won't give people a second chance at honesty. They're either honest or they're dishonest, and if they're dishonest, they're not in my life.

This sounds pretty harsh. But I feel that since there is no shortage of people who will honor you, why even bother with those who don't? So I refuse to lower my expectations of others, even when I see this going on all around me. Human relationships are too important to dishonor.

Lack of Trustworthiness

Related to honesty is trustworthiness. Why is this important? Trust allows you a solid foundation to stand on and to build on. You can be yourself around someone you trust. But how seldom is trust maintained! Look at how intimates of the famous turn around and run to the tabloids to sell stories about their "friends." If you were the person being betrayed, how would you feel?

What does this type of situation tell us? It doesn't tell us a thing about the betrayers. They never really disguised who they were. We shouldn't have those kind of people in our life to begin with. They give us a thousand signals not to trust them and we continue to let them stay. The lesson, then, is not for them. It's for you.

I was thinking recently about Princess Diana having an affair with a man who ran off and sold the story for four million dollars. He's not the problem, though, because he could not have disguised himself. Energy cannot lie. I've never met a person who could tell me a lie where I didn't know they were lying. Nor did you. That's because there's a universal consciousness. Tap into it and all the knowledge that you need is there. It's called intuition. When you trust your intuition you're always right.

Constant Supervision

Are you in a supervised relationship? Supervision means that the other person in the relationship is always controlling you. They ask questions such as, where are you going? Where were you? Who were you with? The supervised person in the relationship adapts to that. Not adapting becomes equated with challenge, and rather than being challenging, with the resultant hassle, the supervised party acquiesces. Basically, you've got a dominant/submissive situation with supervision.

But being dominated violates a person's very essence. The real part of the person starts to burn up inside, thinking, I'm a mature person. I don't need to be supervised. I don't need someone to tell me what to do and when and how to do it.

Remember this: You're an adult. An adult relationship is about two individuals sharing what they find most compatible about each other, without loss of autonomy. Supervision is for children, prison inmates, and certain pets.

Others' Opinions About You

Sure, you should be interested in what other people think about you. To an extent. A very limited one. You see, everybody has an opinion about you, and if you pay too much attention to what others think about you, you start taking a lot of your cues from them. You decide to do or not do something, say or not say something, share or not share. What you do, say, and share can all become based on other people's opinions when you want them to have a good opinion of you.

No matter what you do, though, you're never going to please everybody. And by the time you get around to having enough people liking you, you're not going to like yourself anymore because of all the compromises you have had to make to meet their standards. I'd rather be hated by everybody but loved by myself than be loved by everybody and hate myself.

Manipulative Criticism

Well-thought-out criticism can be a good thing. A problem comes in, though, when criticism is self-serving, and when people add a twist of control onto it. You hear talk of constructive criticism, but there's often a question of exactly what's being constructed, and why. For instance, you're a young artist, happy in what you're doing but struggling financially. Your father tells you you're lazy and lack ambition, that you ought to go to school to get an MBA, and then get a "real" job. Just what is he constructing? A more fulfilling life for you? Or the realization of his image of what a child of his should be?

No one knows you the way you know yourself. No one can know what you're feeling. Many times, others' judgments of you are merely projections of themselves and have nothing to do with who you are. Always question others' judgments about you. Always.

Pain

The Upper West Side of Manhattan seems to attract the intellectual, long-suffering, cloistered minds of the world. You see them in bookstores. You see them in restaurants. You see them in very intense conversation with furrowed brow, leaning forward, pointing in someone's face, pounding on tables, frothing at the mouth. This is where the heart of activism and social commentary is located. There's a lot of pain here.

I'm all for social activism—as one facet of life. But many people take their identity more from their pain than from their pleasure. They believe that their lives are justified by the pain that they feel and exhibit. In fact, they are terrified by the idea that there can be pleasure in life without pain.

We're not comfortable when people enjoy pleasure. If a woman engages in pleasure, we have derogatory names for her. A woman doctor was on my show the other day. She is a gynecologist/obstetrician and a very angry woman. She said that the men in the hospitals where she worked put her down because she displayed pleasure, passion, and creativity in her work. They couldn't handle it.

We're very limited in the amount of pleasure we allow. Pleasure has to be of very short duration and it has to be socially constructed. So it's acceptable to take pleasure in going to church to pray. Or in going on a family vacation—provided that we've truly earned it by working like crazy beforehand, and that it's not too long.

Caretaking

A caretaker is an okay thing to have—on an estate. But not in my adult relationship, please! By caretaking I mean when a person feels that their purpose is to serve you. Everything they do involves making your life better. Implied in their caretaker role is that they don't think you're adult enough to take care of yourself. You're being treated like a child. As in the supervised relationship, you can never be completely independent.

A lot of people base relationships on how much caretaking

they do for their partner. Often it's the woman who assumes or gets assigned this role. Even in the 90s, many women are expected to do all the household chores. So they wash all the dishes, cook all the food, iron all the clothes, sometimes willingly, at least for a while. What would happen if the man were to share those chores? You might have a truly adult relationship.

What do others do for you that you could do for yourself?

Do you look to others too much? List all the things you expect from other people that you could easily do yourself. Think carefully; you may be surprised at the length of your list. Doing this exercise and acting upon it will give you more freedom to be who you are. It will improve your relationships too.

Yes, it's sometimes wonderful to have people do things for us when we don't strictly need them to. The trouble is, we can develop rigid expectations when we ought to be flexible. For instance, husbands often expect wives to do the cooking, and as we just discussed in the previous section, caretaker-oriented wives may be happy to. This is all okay, during those times when it's mutually acceptable. But what if one day you, as the husband, come home and see that your wife has had a hard day, and she's tired? She may not feel well. Will you expect her to fulfill her customary role, or will you take some responsibility for those chores yourself? Or what would happen if you said, "Let's change this. I'll cook one day, you cook the next"? Suddenly, it increases the respect each person has for the other. It acknowledges the other in that moment. It acknowledges the importance of the moment.

If, on the other hand, you say, "Nope; this is the way it is. The woman does this, I do that, period." Then there's no respect, no moment, only something old that's based upon the past that you're living with as if it's unchangeable law. It's fine to live with antiques, but not when they're ideas.

Think of all the women who pick up the clothes and do the laundry just because it's expected of them. Are you one of them? What if you started to say to those you live with, there's no reason why you can't do the laundry, why you can't clean the dishes, why you can't vacuum? I'm a fervent believer in the idea that we should never allow permanency in the way we live. We should have so much flexibility in our life arrangements that we can adjust and change without it seeming like a major trauma in which people start accusing one another. Respect the moment. Things change. Nothing is ever the same.

Do you need or seek approval?

Have you ever been a stamp collector, getting sets of stamps sent to you monthly, "on approval"? If you liked the stamps you could accept and pay for them; if not, you could send them back. The on-approval mode is fine in the hobbyist's world, but some people live their lives like this, offering up their every action for scrutiny by others before they commit themselves to it.

Do you live your life in this tentative, on-approval mode, not really finalizing anything until you've got someone else's go-ahead? For instance, do you dress for someone else? Do you do your hair for others? Or do you do these things for you? When you do things with an eye to approval from other people, you should at least ask yourself if what you are doing is authentic to your own spirit as well.

When you need someone else's approval, you set the stage for problems. You run the risk of not getting the approval you seek or of getting it for a while and then being cut off from it. If you are cut off, you internalize that by feeling a silent sense of betrayal. Then you start to resent the other person.

Sometimes people try to get approval for their pain. What happens if you don't acknowledge that? I'm the last person in the world you should ever complain to because I'll expect you to come up with a solution to your problem and act on it. I believe you can instantaneously tap into every answer you need to be absolutely content, positive, well, happy, balanced, and fulfilled in your life. Allow that in and it will immerse you. That energy is there to be used. Why seek someone else's approval when you already know everything you need to know?

Do you focus on learning or on succeeding?

Learning is more important than succeeding, although not many people seem to think so. Think of all the people who get their MBAs and go out there to succeed without really learning anything. Many of these people spend more than what they earn, living beyond their means in order to show that they are somebody. Their educational, career, and monetary successes teach them nothing. As a result, when they lose any part of it, their whole self-image is diminished.

What if they went out to learn first? Then success would not be important and learning would be. If success occurred it would merely be as a side effect of learning. When I go out to race, it's not important that I win. I can feel just as good coming in last as first, because what I'm most interested in is what I can learn. Every time I train and every time I race, I'm learning. Yes, I have won a lot of races, hundreds of them. But I don't need to remind myself with trophies and plaques because the winning came as a result of what I learned, and it's the learning process that was the most important part of the experience. Another important aspect of it for me is that as a result of what I've learned, I've been able to teach other people. They in turn teach others, and everyone continues to grow.

Think of the mistakes you make because you are more interested in the goal of success than in the learning process. Try getting up in the morning with the attitude of wanting to learn. Ask yourself, what do I want to learn today? That will put your mind and emotions in a whole new stance vis-a-vis that day's activities. If you're only interested in succeeding, you may reach your goal, you may have a conquest of some type, but what will you have learned in the process? Nothing. It will be a hollow success, and you yourself will still feel empty. As a result you'll create more and more goals. You'll never have achieved enough. When you get into the learning mode, by contrast, you don't have to have constant success. You're fulfilled by the learning process.

What messages do you carry with you?

Subconsciously, you carry with you the messages of your childhood. Your personality evolves from these messages. While for some people the messages of early life are positive, involving unconditional love and acceptance, if we've received negative ones they can hobble us later on, without our ever realizing it. Here are some examples of negative messages that children receive. Were some of these transmitted to you?

What you believe is untrue.

As an example, you're 10 years old. Your mother is speaking negatively about someone, and you overhear it. You say, "Mom, what are you talking about?" And she says, "Oh, nothing." Later, you ask, "Did you say something bad about someone?" And she says, "No." But you know that she has. She makes you feel as if what you're hearing and seeing is not true. She has denied your experience.

What you perceive is irrelevant.

Everything is relevant to a young child. Every new discovery becomes a new reality, hence, a new sensation and a new perception. The last thing you should do is tell a child that something is irrelevant. That teaches the child that nothing has importance. If nothing the child discovers has importance, then the only thing that is important is what the mother or father says. This becomes the focus of the child.

As a result, children grow up to become insensitive. They become uninterested in other people's realities. These become irrelevant.

Look at commuters who ride into Manhattan each day from the suburbs. Many go right through slums, not caring. These neighborhoods are irrelevant to them. Many are insensitive to the obviously unemployed around them. These people are irrelevant to them. *They're* not going to lose *their* job.

Do you fall into this pattern? If a friend or family member shares her feelings with you, do you realize that what that person is saying is important to her? Do you really pay attention,

76

and try to understand that person's predicament? If you don't, you may be acting on internalized messages from long ago. If you do, though, you're empowering not just that friend or family member, but yourself.

You can't be trusted.

How many times have you been told that you couldn't be trusted? You weren't responsible? You let people down? Someone immediately corrected you and showed you the right way of doing or saying something. Every time someone did that, you began to feel a certain ineffectualness, an inability to do. That creates helplessness.

How often do you see men showing women how to do things? The woman says, "I don't know how to do this; please show me." This pattern, one that goes back to early training, plays both ways in reinforcing helplessness.

In Sweden, every citizen is required to know how to fix a car engine; otherwise, you could get stranded in the snow there, and die. So men and women, young and old, have to master auto mechanics to get their driver's license. It's a matter of survival.

You are not lovable.

If you buy into this one, you keep people away. Or the people you do allow into your life are the ones who reinforce your self-concept of unlovableness. You find relationships that keep you in constant conflict. In that way, you continue to believe you are undeserving of affection.

You are stupid.

Have you ever been told that you were stupid? Why in the world would someone say that? They must have been frustrated and impatient. They wanted something done immediately. They didn't recognize that we can have different solutions to one problem and all be right. They wanted you to see things their way and to work in their time frame. They wanted you to come up with their solutions. In short, they wanted you to fit into their agenda.

All you need are a few of these "you are stupid" messages at a sensitive age and you start to pull back. You hold back all your vulnerability. You become completely isolated from any sense of a self that is going to be courageous enough to break through and actually do something on your own. Thus, you start to show that you *are* stupid. You won't take any risks or chances, and people believe that you are stupid simply because of what you refuse to do.

Why do you think so many people in our society never take any risks at all, living a passive spectator existence, watching safely from the sidelines as others take the risks? It's because they grew up believing they were stupid, and they are not going to do anything that will bring any more contempt upon them.

You are evil.

Many of us were taught that curiosity about sex is evil, when it is natural. Other cultures explore their bodies without shame, embarrassment, or ridicule. For many children here, though, one of the first admonitions given is not to masturbate. Children are told it is evil, and if they're caught, they're reprimanded, smacked, punished, humiliated.

As a result of our grossly repressed sexuality, we become afraid to explore the depths of our sexual feelings. The moment we do, we have both guilt and fear. We even restrain our capacity to fantasize. We literally block it. Or if we do fantasize, we begin to feel evil and dirty. If, as a child, you were rejected, punished, and ridiculed for wanting to be in touch with your own sexuality, it may not be easy to be sexual as an adult.

Boys and girls don't take risks. Children are seen and not heard.

Here are other messages that live deep within our subconscious. As a result of these, many people keep their true feelings inside. They only talk for utilitarian purposes or to express frustration, never as a way of freeing or empowering themselves. They are silent about the issues they should be discussing and the feelings they should be voicing.

If you feel strongly about something, you should find your voice and talk about the issue. Face it, confront it, and engage it. I see people who will gossip about a situation but not face the issue head-on. To me, that shows they've learned the negative lessons of early childhood too well.

Are you self-empowered?

Being empowered means being in control of your life. When you recognize your own authority, you feel good about yourself. You move at your own pace. You feel full whether or not you are busy. When you are not in charge of your life, on the other hand, you look to other things or people to fill you up. These could be a cult, church, fraternity, sorority, spouse, girlfriend, club, or workplace. The problem here? If you're not self-empowered, their power is likely to supersede your own.

True self-empowerment is not mirrored in worldly power, success, wealth, or possessions. It's mirrored in your manner of living, because true empowerment is accompanied by a sense of inner peace. You know where you should be and what you should be doing. I've met truck drivers, farmers, schoolteachers, and other people in all areas of life who feel completely in balance. They are empowered and feel good about themselves. Empowerment gives them an inner direction; other people can't sway them.

Empowerment is the actualization of your potential. Most people intellectualize about what they should be doing instead of living up to their abilities. When you are empowered, though, you live your life the way you need to live it—you don't just talk about it. You do what you know you essentially need to be doing.

The movie *Forrest Gump* showed a man who was self-empowered. He always did what he believed in. He ran back and forth across the country because he felt that was what he should be doing. Other people followed him for the wrong reasons. They thought that if Forrest did it, they should do it. They were copycats. Unlike the others, Forrest was always motivated from within himself. He acted out of his beliefs in everything he did, from playing ping-pong to running a shrimp boat to going to war.

Look at your own life. What don't you like about yourself? Think of the things you do that you are not happy about. Be aware of what you think, say, and do that disempowers you. In fact, write down what you think, say, and do in a day. How do these things make you feel? Are they empowering or disempowering? If you feel disempowered, what can you do to change the situation to enhance your well-being?

If you were to draw a blueprint for a new life, what would it look like?

Let's say you were starting over today from scratch. What would a blueprint for your life look like?

You can start over at any point in your life. In my running and walking group I meet many people who are beginning to turn their lives around, and believe me, there is no right age to do this. Rather, there is no *wrong* age; they're all right! Harry, for instance, is 81 and he just started changing his life at 79. He gave up his friends because they were talking about death and disease and he didn't want to engage in that. He chose to re-engage in life and to start running marathons. Harry became the architect of his life.

I'm suggesting that you can start out fresh today. To do this you must be willing to change your perceptions about life. You must realize that you are in control. You make life happen; life is not something that happens to you.

There are three important stages in the process. Let's go through them.

Imagine your ideals.

Visualize your new life as if it already exists. Ask yourself, what do I want in my life? See a picture of it in your mind. Write about it and look at what you've written. Don't edit your description. Believe that anything is possible, because it is. Recently, for the first time in American history, a 63-year-old woman won an award for being the outstanding athlete of the year for all age groups. The first time I met her, seven years before that, she could hardly lift a weight or run up stairs. She persevered toward her goal because she had a vivid dream in her mind of what she could do. What she saw allowed her to keep on going.

You need to start with an idealistic image. Don't be afraid of having ideals in a society that has so few.

Take practical steps.

After you create an image of what you desire, determine the steps you will take to get there. Then, give yourself a timetable. As an example, I'm currently working on a new project, an organic farm in Florida. I visualize a cooperative venture with a lot of people participating. I see a 10- to 15-acre farm with lots of gardens. In the middle of this farm is a big, beautiful 1800s-style general store. There is a large organic health food store. People can walk through a kitchen behind glass and see food being freshly made, everything from Essene breads baking to sprouts being grown. There are also greenhouses where hydroponics are grown, gardens with exotic flowers from all over the Americas, a restaurant, and a crafts center. I see all this.

To make it happen, I must see this developing in stages. I have an architect drawing my plans. The project will take three years to complete.

You have to know how to stage your life. When you see what you ideally want, where you want to be, what you want to be doing, and whom you want to be with, plan it out in stages. Don't jump ahead of yourself. Don't expect big changes to occur too quickly. Take your time. Work on it gradually, and give yourself a lot of leeway. Don't overstress yourself.

Get support.

Share your plans with people who support you. Telling your story is like a rite of passage because making a transition is always significant and talking about it to others strengthens your commitment to change. Giving voice to your ideas makes them more real. They're no longer just a little secret in your head that nobody knows about.

Bring the significant people in your life together. Invite them to lunch or dinner. (Note: Don't invite the habitual naysayers to this particular meal. You know who they are!) Share with your supporters where you are at in your life. Telling your story is so important; never assume that it's not of interest. So tell it. Explain to people what works for you and what doesn't. Then show them where your life is going and how you are going to get there. Let them know what role you would like them to play in your life. You want people to celebrate your change. You are saying: I'm changing, here is what I'm doing, and here is what I need. People who really support you will love that! And you will love their response.

Note this too: If it should be the case that at this particular juncture in your life, you have no supporters, that happens sometimes. Don't abort your plans because of this circumstance. Remember that believing in yourself is really the most important thing by far.

In order to believe that you can do anything, first, you must believe in your completeness.

A lot of people believe that they are going to change their lives. They want to change them, and they have good ideas about what they want to do. But nothing changes. Part of the reason that nothing really changes is that they don't see themselves as complete enough to engage in the change. You have to be complete to engage in change. It's the completeness that gives you the ability to go forward. In the absence of completeness, only fragmented parts of the self venture forward.

Only from your sense of completeness and the totality of your being do you go forward with meaning. When you allow the complete self out, everything becomes a point of excitement. Have you ever watched a child? They see something new and they become excited. They're so complete. It's the totality of the child that responds. They've involved themselves totally in the excitement of discovery because they have no fear.

I am complete enough to do anything at any time, anywhere that I choose. I can be what I want to be. I am whole and have everything I need. Every recipe I need to make my life work is here within me. And the same is true for you.

Becoming the Hero in Your Own Life

5

5

Over the years I've helped thousands of people prepare themselves for participation in marathons. And of course I've trained for numerous marathons myself. It's an amazing process, one that never ceases to inspire me, because it affects all aspects of one's being. In fact, I'd say that a marathon runner's training is more than the sum of all its individual parts. It's more than vitamins, diet, exercise, stress management, and guided visualization. All these components have a place, but none of them embody the heart of it. At the core of training, we learn what it means to live life as a hero.

We're living in a time plagued with dysfunction, much of which is self-inflicted. We hear people whine, moan, blame, and complain. We witness people who relish being victims when they don't have to be victims.

In running and racewalking you see the healthier side of the coin. You see a woman on crutches with multiple sclerosis making it to the finish line. Long after everyone else has finished the race she pushes onward, cold and fatigued, without the cheering fans and without the water stops.

Such a courageous accomplishment demonstrates that we

can do amazing things when we are determined and when our hearts are in what we do. We start to realize that our pain and blisters are not so bad when we see others reaching seemingly insurmountable goals.

Over the years, I have had the opportunity to run and communicate with athletes from countries the world over. People explain to me their rationale for training and talk about what keeps them going. The theme that emerges is one of becoming the hero in your own life.

I have met many heroes. Such people are easy to identify. They do not feel the need to draw attention to themselves. Nor do they brag about their accomplishments or conquests. Heroes are often quiet people who engage in life rather than talk about it. They choose to work rather than to talk and they don't feel the need to engage in debates to convince you that their point of view is the right one.

Doing the marathon is an enormous challenge for many people, one that can be terrifying. Think of running or racewalking for 26 miles, alone. This is not a team sport. You do it with other people but it's a uniquely individual process. At times you feel that you can't do it but at the very same moment something in you says, yes, I can. You go through the fear, absorb it, let it go, and then become transformed at the end of the process.

Heroics in this sport is well exemplified in the movie *On the Edge*, with Bruce Dern. This is about a great athlete, one of America's best, who tries out for the Olympics. Due to dirty politics on the part of some competitors, he becomes disqualified and is barred from ever competing again.

Almost ten years go by before he decides that yes, he will compete again. He chooses a famous run that takes place on a murderous course in San Francisco. The course is extremely hilly; it goes straight up a gigantic hill and then straight down. I ran that course and found it to be the toughest course I ever ran in my life.

The athlete comes to town and trains every day. He has almost no money but rents a room in town and devotes all his time to his task. Each day he marks off the days till the race on his calendar, and each night he records his progress in a diary. The man seems to have no life outside of his training. His only purpose appears to be to redeem his reputation.

During this arduous process, he meets a wise, old athletic coach, who tells him that he is training all wrong; he is not training with his heart but with anger. The coach advises him not to run to prove people wrong but for the love of what he is doing. In effect, he is turning a negative situation into a positive one through a change in focus.

From that point on, Bruce Dern begins to train with full investment of his mind and heart. You can immediately see the transformation in him.

The day of the race is beset with obstacles. His nemesis, the person who disqualified him ten years earlier, is again one of the race's sponsors. At first Dern is able to hide from him but later on, in the middle of the race when he starts to gain, he is noticed. The sponsor does everything in his power to stop him. He calls the police and asks them to prevent Dern from getting over the top of the hill.

Just before that happens, the other runners realize what is going on and begin to protect him. Now no one is able to stop him. At the end of the course, Dern actually breaks free and is in the lead. Just before crossing the finish line, though, he pulls

Becoming the Hero in Your Own Life

back and joins hands with the other runners. They all cross the finish line together.

An athlete immediately associates with the heroism in this movie. But anyone can. And let's broaden the picture to understand that not everyone has to run a marathon to be a hero. There are life experiences that are the character-proving equivalent of crossing the finish line. In fact, there's a good chance you already have gone through at least one. Maybe it was a risky job change that you made, or a relationship breakup that you struggled to get through. Maybe it was an academic degree that you worked years to attain, an illness that you overcame, or a move that you made to a strange city. Whatever it was, if you've gone out and met the challenge you know that you don't have to fear that kind of challenge any more. You've proved that you have the inner strength to deal with it. So you may already be a hero without realizing it.

Realize it.

What do you do when you are dissatisfied with your life?

If you are like many people, you try to compensate for your dissatisfaction by distracting yourself from it. Instead of thinking through your situation and working toward change, you distract yourself through escapist endeavors. You may watch TV excessively, or overeat. You may gamble or take drugs. You may get into bad relationships or become overly responsible for others. In short, you do something that takes you away from yourself. So you become too busy to ever think about being a hero. You seem to sneak though the days, just managing to get by, instead of really living your life. Time goes by and you take no journey, you learn no lesson, you leave no legacy.

How does that change? It changes when you learn to be yourself. Being yourself will make you a hero in your own life.

Is there something you would love to do but fear trying?

For example, have you ever thought about writing a book or about engaging in some other form of creative expression? What stops you from doing that?

You think it would take too much time.

Perhaps you think that writing a book takes too much time. What gives you this impression? An average book contains approximately between 20,000 to 100,000 words. That's about twice or three times the words than many people say in a day. When you put it into that perspective, writing a book is really not such a big deal, is it?

Learn to put whatever you're afraid of trying into a new perspective.

You're not focused on personal goals.

Perhaps you're not accustomed to working for yourself. I talked to a typist who believed she could never write a book, yet every day she typed a hundred pages for other people. Working at that rate for herself she could have typed a major manuscript in a week's time. Of course she would have had to write original material as well, but the point is that she was not in the habit of choosing where to focus her energy.

You fear not being accepted.

None of us is accepted by everyone. In fact, many of us are intimately acquainted with the experience of nonacceptance. For example, artists aren't accepted by many people in mainstream society. Neither are gay people, African Americans, or liberals.

Worrying about who is going to accept you is a waste of time. You are who you are; why be unsure about yourself? Why look for validation out there instead of attuning yourself to your own values? Why aspire to society's values instead of asserting your own?

The moment you give over your power in that way, you lose control of your life. Now I'm not advocating acting irresponsibly. And I'm not condoning people's flaunting themselves or become exaggerated exhibitionists. That's not balanced. I'm talking about not being fearful that what you are is insufficient. I'm talking about not needing someone else to validate you before you believe you're okay.

Remember, no two people will have the same thoughts and perceptions of you. And no one will ever know you the way you know yourself. You can give away your power of self-validation or you can claim it. Two powers cannot share the same space with equal intensity at the same time—this is a dynamic law of physics. So to the degree that you need someone else to accept you, you have given away your own life. Taking back the power is how you regain the strength to become a hero.

In short, you can only be a hero once you stop being concerned about what everyone else thinks. Heroes don't do things for other people's adulation or respect. Being a hero is a quiet, essentially solitary process.

You fear failure.

A person who fears failing is often a person who was told, especially early in life, that they are a failure. When people are repeatedly told things like, "You can't do it right; let me do it for you," that transgresses their intellectual sanctity and eventually distorts their perception of themselves.

The moment someone disempowers you that way, you begin to feel stupid. Soon you begin to believe that you can't accomplish anything. It takes effort then to turn your self-image around.

What opportunities did you let go because you doubted you could handle them?

Chances are that beliefs you have accepted as real have kept you from doing things. As a result, opportunities came and went. You may have had many opportunities, but if you didn't have confidence at that moment, they disappeared. Then you have regrets. You think, "What if?" The other part of you says, "But you didn't."

Heroes greet opportunities head-on, and embrace them. So make this mental note to yourself:

Think before you let the next opportunity slip by, because the day will come when you won't have any more. Of course one way to increase the number of opportunities that present themselves is to have a positive outlook. Positive people have far more opportunities because they make them every day. A positive person's mind is constantly open, and the nice thing about being open and free is that there's no limit to the opportunities you create for yourself. I've never met a creative, open, healthy person who didn't have far more ideas than what they could achieve in four lifetimes.

The person who falls back on the predictable "I can't" mindset loses out. Every opportunity goes right by that individual. The person may flirt with an opportunity, be tempted by it, or even sample it, but not embrace it. There's a big difference there.

Can you embrace challenge?

Think of a time when you've embraced challenge, even though you were scared to death of it. Has there been such a time? If so, you'll probably long remember every detail of it. You may even savor those memories too.

I think back to a day in Maine a couple of years ago. That was when a group of friends and I went whitewater rafting, which is one great trip, if you're up for some cold water and a few adrenaline surges. Several of my friends had never shot rapids before. As they got settled into the raft, their bodies were stiff, and you could tell they were terrified.

I asked them if they wanted to do this.

Yes, we want to do this! they said. Even though we're scared to death, we want to do this!

There were only about three minutes of preparation, during which we learned how to position our bodies in the boat, what to do if we got thrown out of it, and how to get back in. It was like Survival 101—The Crash Course—condensed.

On calm water, you can't imagine how rough it might get just around the bend. You simply can't. However, preparing your mind for the eventuality does help; in fact, it makes all the difference. So, while you're still in calm water, you review mentally what you will have to do when turbulence hits: Lean forward—lean into the boat, and paddle like hell. Keep a complete sense of focus and keep your body relaxed enough so that your own rigidity doesn't throw you against somebody else or throw you out of the boat. We *had* been paying attention during those three minutes.

The calm was short-lived; it took only one turn and turbid water hit. Waves and swells that seemed 10 feet high assaulted us. Then, almost before we knew what was happening, we went into a kind of combination water hole and wave, and our raft was—for want of a more accurate term—underwater.

Why had we done this? This was really dangerous! Through the little spaces of air that were somehow still around us came the words, "Paddle like hell!"

Yes, we knew what to do! We were already doing it—leaning forward, into the boat, paddling like hell. We kept a complete sense of focus and kept our bodies relaxed enough so that our own rigidity didn't throw us against somebody else or out of the boat. Thus we came up above the wave and out of the water hole.

Everybody clapped and cheered! We all high-fived each other, because clearly, we had discovered an exciting new level of potential in ourselves. Some of my friends' lives were profoundly changed then, and—I find this truly amazing—it had taken only 5 or 6 seconds for that to happen.

What these friends now understood was that the category of what they could experience and achieve was a much vaster one than they'd assumed. They'd delved deeper into the possibilities of their lives, by overcoming fears and going out to meet a new challenge. Now, they knew that they'd never find themselves walking along the river's edge, wondering if they could survive the rapids. They'd already mastered them.

My friends talked about "that big wave" for days. "What about that big wave!" was practically the only thing they could say for a long time after the trip. It was as if they were fascinated by that wave. But they knew it wasn't that particular wall of water itself that was so enchanting—it was their own strength in coming through it. Maybe they could even go on to become the heroes in their own lives.

We complete many obstacle courses in life.

People are usually open about what they can't do, but they're less willing to acknowledge, especially to themselves, what they *can* do. For instance, most people develop all kinds of coping skills over the years, albeit often out of necessity. I believe that practically everyone who's made it as far as adulthood has done things in life that are far more difficult than negotiating some rapids or running a marathon. Have you lost a loved one? Lost a job? Been in a good relationship that went bad and felt the pain of getting out of it? As we mentioned earlier, these are the kinds of situations that mold and reveal heroes.

But unlike whitewater rafting adventures or marathons, these situations don't get resolved in a few hours. They take months or years to get through. It takes an enormous amount of courage to get past them, but once you grieve and let go, you become stronger for it.

Give yourself credit, then, for what you have gone through. Acknowledge as many positive traits about yourself as you can. That will remind you that you're not just starting this journey toward heroism today; you've been engaged in it for a long time.

How do you respond to ineptitude?

What's your most common response to ineptitude? You probably judge it. You're most likely critical, and condemn yourself or others for it. But what would happen if, instead of condemning ineptitude, you intervened in a nonjudgmental way to try to help the inept person? This is particularly important when that person is yourself!

Think of yourself as a coach instead of an athlete. The first thing a coach has to do is to empathize with what the athlete is going through. Isn't it more constructive to work with a person by saying, "Let's see if we can't together figure out a better way of doing this?" Then, you engage the person in problem-solving instead of making the person feel as if they're the problem. Again, if *you're* the one you're coaching, this is particularly important.

Learn to turn off the critical mind that tends to have knee-jerk reactions to anything it doesn't want to deal with. Give yourself and others the benefit of the doubt. Try taking a step back, disengaging the ego, and dealing with the situation honestly and openly in a constructive way. With that attitude you are sure to find solutions.

What would you change if every act was a measure of your character?

Actually, every act is. But what if every act of yours was made known? Would you act in the same way as usual, or would you change? Imagine a screen above your head allowing the public to see everything you did. Everything about you would suddenly be known.

Examining your life as if that was how you had to live it is one way to keep yourself on a positive emotional and spiritual path.

Here's an even better way: Forget about the public viewing that screen. Imagine *yourself* viewing and critiquing it.

How do you respond to conflict?

I'll always remember the time I was walking down the street with an accomplished martial arts master when we noticed a "wolf pack" of young toughs approaching in our direction. My first instinct was to meet the attack head-on, an approach to physical threat that had worked for me in the past. But my companion insisted that we do a meditation instead. I knew he could have stopped all of the guys single-handedly if he had wanted to; he had that much energy. So I wondered, why use meditation at such a time?

I followed his lead, though, and sure enough, this gang walked around us as if we didn't exist. Never in my life had I experienced anything like that. I knew it wasn't because of me, because I was in fear and ready to fight. I knew it had to do with my companion's simple technique, which involved sending out energy.

I came out of that experience with the understanding that you needn't go head to head with anyone. I had learned something about the ego, about how surrendering it can sometimes be the heroic thing to do. Of course, such training takes years and years before it can successfully be put into practice. But knowing the method exists makes it worth striving for.

Learning to approach conflict—or anything else—in a new way necessitates giving up old ways of thinking and being. You have to give something up before you can take in something new.

Are you a warrior hero?

Historically, we've associated military warriors with heroes. There are nonviolent warriors too, though. The nonviolent warrior is the person who is determined, who fights for something significant, and who represents the best in humanity. Think of people who champion causes and challenge evils, inadequacies, and injustices. Think of the Ralph Naders and Mother Teresas of the world, and of all the people working for similar causes.

Ideally, you should seek your warrior energy while you are still young, healthy, and growing. But some people evolve into warriors only after going through a lot of pain, as a result of being hurt, disempowered, or made ill. At some point, their hurt, pain, and victimization become anger.

That's all right, but you don't want to let anger turn into rage, causing you to lash out. You want to become strong and to grow from your experience, and then use your anger constructively to tap into the warrior hero, the part of you that will go out there and take action.

Can you be a warrior hero over the long haul?

If you are looking to improve the quality of your life, one of your highest aspirations is to become one with life. To be at peace allows you the balance to commit yourself to issues without becoming absorbed by them. When a group called Nader's Raiders started, it consisted of 500 young lawyers and activists. Within three months their numbers dwindled to 20. Today only a handful are left.

Why do people lose their initial drive? It happens when they don't have a sense of peace and balance. These qualities are needed before you can commit yourself to a cause over a long span of time.

Expending energy without being at peace causes you to become burned out. You get involved in ego conflicts and overwhelmed by the challenges you take on. When you see that everything is not going to become righted by your activism, you manifest the opposite extreme by becoming apathetic and giving up.

Do you hesitate to engage in your dreams?

Do you dream about something all the time but fail to engage in it? What do you have that's so important that you're afraid of losing it? Why do you hold on to old habits? How do they serve you?

If you investigate these questions you'll probably find that many habits give you the illusion of stability and comfort, but not true satisfaction. They keep you limited and bored, but you hold on to them because they make your life predictable. If you value the known you probably fear challenge and the uncertainty of taking risks.

The hero has no certainties. Where they're going, what will happen, how they'll feel—these are unknowns. But that's how life should be lived. Life is always most exciting when you're on the edge, when you have absolutely no certainty that the next step is not going to throw you into an abyss, into darkness, chaos, and crisis. That's when you pay the most attention.

What if, on a day-to-day basis, you could live in such a way? You would always be challenging yourself, always taking risks. You would constantly engage yourself in something instead of always seeking safety behind the conformity of rituals, patterns, and dogmas. Living on the edge would help you to see more clearly. You wouldn't be involved in fantasy.

Reality is always richer than fantasy. But the average American lives more with illusion than with reality. I say this in the sense that we're very image-conscious. The clothes we wear, the jobs and houses and cars we have, where we live, and even our friends, are often components of illusions we're trying to project to tell people who we are. We're normal, we're trying to tell people through these things. We're regular folks.

What if you didn't do that? What if the only way that you could tell people who you were was by the good deeds that you did, the challenges that you took, and the risks you faced? It takes no courage to be normal. Normal is not where heroes live.

Do you have to win at sports, or in other aspects of your life?

Knowing how to exercise discipline, whether you win or lose, allows you to feel like a winner. Actually, I myself don't think in winner or loser terms anymore. That's why I no longer enter marathons to race them; I enter simply to run. My joy comes from running with other people and helping them to get through. It's so enjoyable when you don't have to prove something by racing.

The same holds true for other activities in life. Can you imagine how different the world would be if people believed they didn't have to compete with one another, and cooperated instead? What a difference that would make. We wouldn't be exploited. We wouldn't have the haves and have-nots. We wouldn't have the gross disparities in wealth.

"In hoc signo vinces" (in this sign thou shalt conquer).

Throughout history, groups of people from all walks of life have recognized those amongst them who have taken a step in a different direction. Most individuals, however, hide their differences. They're afraid to stand out in a crowd and even to project differences in a relationship with one other person. They are afraid they will be scorned for their differences, and therefore choose to hide vital parts of themselves.

But by compromising yourself in order to be accepted, you're paying a really high price. You've got to hide your passions, dreams, inspirations, and ideals. Is it worth doing all this just to be accepted?

The hero and the warrior never compromise, nor do they care if they're accepted.

Ten minutes before going to sleep, think about how you can be more of who you are. Think of how different your life could be if you stopped worrying about being accepted. What would you change? What ideals would you live by? What would it feel like to be the hero in your own life?

The next morning, you can find out.

Issues of
Interest to
Women

And The Feminine Side
Of Men

*Put aside your fears and
create change just for the joy
of it. You can take action
from a positive stance.*

6

Are you fulfilled in life?

Evaluate the important areas of your life to determine if your needs are being met. These areas may include:

- Career
- Children
- Play

Career

Your career needs may include satisfaction, recognition, contribution, creativity, self-esteem, money, freedom, accomplishment, growth, connections, bonding and joy. Write these needs down. Above all, a career must honor your real needs and honor you as a human being.

Children

Do you and your children communicate your needs to each other? Perhaps your teenage children need a space that's exclusively their own, where you enter only by invitation. And you, as a parent, may need the same. Explain the concepts of private time and communal time to your children so that everyone's needs are met.

Also, recognize that you must make the transition from parent to friend if you are to have a lifelong relationship with your children. When your child begins to establish mature friendships, it's important that you be included as one of those friends. The parents who are friends with their teenagers are the ones who remain friends for life.

Play

Let's not forget that the serious side of life needs to be balanced by the lighter moments. The ability to play adds tremendous quality to our lives. We always remember the fun we have had and rarely remember the work we have done. So why should we have such little fun?

Do you feel empowered?

List the areas of your life in which you feel you are powerful. Do you make use of that power? If so, in what way? Also, consider the areas of your life in which you do not feel powerful. If you express power at work but not at home, write that down. What does this mean to you? To understand these distinctions, delve into your past to review how your patterns of power developed. When and where did you start to feel disempowered? By retracing these events, you can restore your power in all areas of your life.

What lessons can your inner little girl teach you now?

When little girls reach the age of seven, eight or nine, they have a natural desire to explore the world. They want to do things just for the sake of doing them. They want to explore the world just because it is there. The little girl is no different from the little boy in this respect. All children possess a natural assertiveness and a desire for self-expression.

Every little girl is also a magician, what Robert Bly refers to as a "mythical trickster." This quality allows the girl to change. She weaves fantasies, illusions and spells into her life that allow her to be absolutely anything. Then, as she is taught to follow cultural prescriptions for being a "nice girl," she starts to shut down. In our culture's training of males, curiosity is a positive value. Boys and men are encouraged to investigate the world around them. Curious females are often called "nosey" and are encouraged to stay close to home. They are trained not to ask impolite questions about what lies behind appearances. They begin to ignore and shut down the natural intuitive abilities that lead them to question.

If you were not valued for yourself during your early years, you were doubly discouraged. Was your parents' attention contingent upon your being or acting a particular way? Perhaps you were noticed only when you were intelligent, or when you made your parents laugh, and otherwise you were ignored. If so, some aspects of your personality will have become unduly exaggerated while others will have been ignored. You must recover the rejected parts of yourself.

Specific family pressures may have caused you to become overly attuned to others and underattuned to your own instincts. For example, a parent who was unavailable due to absence, depression or alcoholism may have been unable to enjoy your company or support your endeavors, giving you the impression that you are unlovable and ineffective. Perhaps you were forced into an adult role such as surrogate mother for younger siblings, which further required you to ignore your own feelings and fantasies. Regardless of how difficult your life circumstances have been, you can begin at any time to reignite your pleasure in being alive.

Right now, no matter what your age or circumstances, you can rekindle the dreams of your girlhood and learn to honor your instinctive self. If you can ignore your conditioning, you will discover that your curiosity is still alive and that you have inner guidance and resources that will show you how to feel alive. When you allow your thinking to be energized by your instincts and your intuitions, you can do anything in the world you want. Dream your dreams and your inner guides will show you how to accomplish the impossible.

How can you do this? Start by letting yourself imagine what would give you joy in your life (in work, relationships and other important areas). If you draw a blank, recall the times when you felt most excited and happy as a child. What were you doing? What were you thinking of doing? What would you have liked to be doing? Bring those dreams back. The child inside you will guide your fantasies and allow you to feel playful and spontaneous. Other archetypal inner figures—your trickster, your heroine, your wild woman—will give you clues about how to carry them out. They will suggest new directions for you to explore and tell you how your life is out of balance.

To make contact with your guides, pay attention to your

dreams and practice listening to your intuition. Ignore inner voices that are critical, controlling or competitive—the voices that discourage intuition. Be curious. Find the courage to be conscious of what you see and hear.

How important is autonomy to you?

Women, for the most part, have been conditioned to derive their identity from their relationships. While relationships are important, true inner identity must be maintained as well. You must nurture yourself before you can become part of a healthy relationship. Life is an inner journey that each of us must take alone. Establish boundaries for yourself that allow you to collect your thoughts and identify who you are.

In your journal, record your thoughts on the importance of having time and space to yourself. In what areas of your life are you fiercely autonomous? In what areas do you need to develop more autonomy?

What are you doing that is vital and energizing?

Vitality is not something we occasionally need in our lives. Every single day should be life-affirming. List the aspects of your daily life that are vital.

What in your life represents gender compliance?

You must begin to recognize patterns that affect your well-being. Examine each area of your life to determine if you are compliant because you are a woman, or if you are able to participate as an equal. Do you do things just because they are "required" of you in your role as a woman? Are you in a pattern of continual compliance merely because of your sex?

Avoid taking compliant, role-model positions in life that conflict with your inner feelings. When you do something, let it be because you get joy from it, not because it is a form of gender compliance. Does your husband expect you to perform household chores after work because it is your role? That doesn't make sense, and it may prevent you from actualizing who you really are.

Do you trust your own values, perceptions and needs?

Many people find it difficult to follow their personal calling because they feel pressured to fulfill the expectations of others. Should you venture off in a new direction and fail, you will be reminded over and over again of your failure. You may even be told that you are selfish because you disappointed others who depend on you.

Consider this example: A friend of mine gave up a secure job as an accountant after 22 years to start his own business, even though he wasn't sure that he would succeed. His family was terribly angry because his decision threatened their sense of security. They tried to undermine him and eventually succeeded. Within a year, their lack of confidence in him and his own uncertainty got him into serious trouble. He made some bad business decisions and finally had to sell his home. His family blamed him for being a failure.

I talked with his children one day. I asked them if their father had ever acted like a hero and they said no. I then asked them to define what a hero was. They said that a hero was a person who took risks. "Didn't their father take a risk?" I asked. They agreed that he had. "Isn't he a hero then?" I asked. They told me they had never thought of it in that way before. I reminded them that their father was willing to take a chance and start over again at the age of 50. I also pointed out that their father's experience gave them the chance to start over again and to learn that less is more. It gave them a chance to spend more time together as a family. Before, their father had always worked at night to earn extra money for the mortgage.

The children began to appreciate this concept. What changed was not the reality of their situation. They still didn't have any money. But their perception of not having money changed. No longer did they view themselves as failures.

Look at the times in your life when you took a chance. Acknowledge yourself for taking these risks and note the positive lessons that came from these experiences.

What truths have you yet to explore or actualize?

You have truths in you that need to be explored and expressed. What are they? These feelings come from your heart, and you need to write them down. The key to your diary is not to think about what you plan to write, but just to begin writing. Don't let the conditioned part of yourself edit your original thoughts. Doubts will creep in and deter you from the truth you need to express. You may know inside that you want to change careers, for example, but your conditioned responses may tell you that you don't have the education or that you have too many responsibilities to meet and bills to pay.

Put your immediate thoughts down on paper. Look at them, feel them, let them ferment. That's how change starts. It's a difficult process, but you must allow yourself to face harsh truths about your life—what you have given up, the inadequacies of your relationships, the feelings of personal or spiritual emptiness. Perhaps you would rather not let yourself know about these things, but you will feel much stronger and more powerful when you become truthful with yourself and those around you.

Your hidden personal truth includes positive things about yourself, such as talents you've never acknowledged. Perhaps you have a good singing voice that you've been too self-conscious to develop.

What goals have you achieved, and how have they affected you?

Don't look for change to happen all at once. Life is lived in small measures. Every day, small things come together that work. If you think you haven't achieved much in life, you may not be acknowledging all the little things you have done that add up to major accomplishments. Remember that small goals are the essence of life; they validate us.

Write down the small goals you have accomplished. How did you feel when you achieved them? What did they mean to you? If one of your goals was to exercise every day and you went out and did it, that's a goal accomplished. How do you feel? What patterns changed because you accomplished your goal? You may realize that after four months of daily exercise, you began to reprioritize your schedule and make more time for yourself. Perhaps you never realized how much time you were giving to others until you began to satisfy your need to exercise. Allotting time to yourself for exercising may make you

111

feel better emotionally, physically and spiritually. Your confidence may improve, allowing you to gain control in other ways. So you see, one pattern leads to another pattern, which leads to the process of change.

What goals have you set but not yet reached?

Consider why you have failed to reach certain goals. In some cases, the reason may be that other people who want to maintain the status quo deter you from your goals. Maybe you become sidetracked by feelings of guilt. One woman came to my running club for two months, for example, and then stopped suddenly. It seemed that her family resented her absence, even though she was only gone three hours a week. They wanted her to be there exclusively for them, and they certainly didn't want her to take charge of any part of her life. They felt threatened by their loss of control over her every moment, even though she was losing weight, feeling good, having new insights and making positive changes. This woman felt tremendous guilt. If she allowed herself to change any further, she feared she might not know how to control her life and things might never be the same.

Well, of course things will never be the same. Yesterday is not like today, and you can't control tomorrow. But look at the reasons why you haven't fulfilled some of your goals. Don't be afraid to negotiate new arrangements when your needs count.

Female social conditioning, early family circumstances and genetic inheritance can make women extremely sensitive to other people's feelings. While your sensitivity can be a positive quality in some circumstances, it can also rule your life in a very negative way if you let it. To be fully alive, you must remain open to change. Women often feel that it is their job to maintain stability at home by never making changes or doing anything that would upset their families. That attitude doesn't help anyone. What you need to do is to remain emotionally connected and attached to your children while allowing change to happen. They will learn flexibility and joy in their own lives by watching you. It is your choice to emphasize your feelings of guilt or to tolerate the guilt you feel in the name of growth for yourself and, ultimately, for those close to you.

What goals have you done nothing about?

List the goals that you have not yet begun to pursue. What seems to be causing the delay? Acknowledging that you have these goals will begin the process of change. It also helps you to understand why you have avoided these goals until now.

Don't berate yourself for having trouble getting started, but stick with the effort. In particular, don't be frightened off by feelings such as depression that may turn up when you start to let go of old patterns. You are mourning the loss of your old self, but you know that the change must take place.

Are your needs realistic, or are they dictated by society?

Do you really desire the things that others expect you to pursue? If your needs stem from a traditional upbringing, rather than your real self, they will prove to be burdensome and unfulfilling. For example, you may think you need to own a home and all the trappings, including a mortgage, because your parents have instilled this desire in you. In reality, however, the economics of owning a home have changed in recent years. There are no guarantees that you will be able to make your mortgage payments in the present economy. Therefore, you must ask yourself if owning a home is a realistic need.

Evaluate all of your needs to determine whether they are realistic.

Are your needs reasonable or are they conditional?

Define your real needs. Consider whether they are being compromised. If you earn an attractive salary but your work conditions are hazardous, your basic need for safety is not being met. In this society, we have been conditioned to believe that if the money is sufficient, then issues such as job safety and satisfaction don't count. Don't be afraid to assert your needs, and don't accept conditions that compromise them.

Are you looking for fulfillment from your relationships?

Do you look for partners who can make you feel more complete? Do you expect others to make you feel good about who you are? If so, you may be in a pattern of co-dependency. It's one thing to appreciate and be attracted to a person whose life "works." It's another to be drawn to such a person because your life does not work and you hope to fix it through your association with this person. That's the wrong reason to be drawn into a relationship.

In healthy relationships in which the partners share their

114

energy, one accepts the other unconditionally. He does not try to change you, control you or manipulate you. When such conditions start to surface, it's time to say good-bye.

Evaluate your relationships honestly. In each instance, consider whether you have an unhealthy need to be with the other person. Are you there because of co-dependency, or are you there because you have something to share?

Is your time spent meeting your own or other people's needs?

Make a list of all the needs you meet on a given day. Determine which needs are your own and which are other people's. Beyond that, which needs are necessary and which are not? Use this list to identify any imbalances in your life. An honest evaluation will show you where your life isn't working and reveal which needs are most pertinent to your life.

Without this list, you may never know where you spend your time. Talking on the telephone and watching television, for example, may drain time and energy that would be better spent on yourself. Get right down to the nitty gritty; look at everything you do every day for yourself and others.

Are you a caretaker? How does this role affect you?

Many people believe that others can't survive without them, and they spend an inordinate amount of time in a caretaking role. How much time do you devote to taking care of other people? With whom do you play this role, and under what conditions? If you spend too much time and energy taking care of others, it may be wise to reconsider your relationship with these people.

Do you try to manipulate the feelings or attitudes of others?

Think of the ways you are dishonest and manipulative in your dealings with others. Do you perceive situations and relationships as they truly are or, rather, the way you want to see them? If something's not right in your life, say so. Then determine how you will fix it. You must accept that some aspect of your life does not work before you can change it. If you deny that the situation exists, it will only get worse. It's manipulative to be dishonest about your attitudes and feelings and how they affect others. If I have a friend who is very sick, I'm going to tell him he's very sick. But I will also tell him I'm there for him if he wants my help.

Do you alter your communications to please others?

In certain relationships, you may modify what you say to gain acceptance. Your words and feelings are at odds because you are withholding your true opinions. This makes you uncomfortable with yourself. Take note of the things you say that conflict with your true feelings. Ask yourself, am I communicating in this way to gain this person's approval? What is the worst that could happen if I expressed myself honestly and this person did not accept me? In the end, you do not want to be in relationship with someone who cannot accept a difference of opinion.

How often are you overcome with fear, anxiety, depression or guilt?

All of these emotions merely cover up our insecurities. They result from a lack of full empowerment in our lives. There was a time in America when most people took responsibility for their own lives. There was very little litigation because people generally didn't accuse others when their lives did not work. In recent times, however, it has become fashionable to blame others for our own shortcomings—anything not to blame ourselves.

Examine all areas of your life to determine where you are blaming others for your failures. Stop the accusations and start looking to yourself for the answers. That's the only way you will find a solution to your problems. When you blame others, you give away your power to them. As a result, you never resolve the issues at hand and go forward with your life.

Are you still denying your real needs?

Think about what you really want from yourself and your friendships. Are your expectations of yourself too low? Make a list of them. You will feel dissatisfied if you haven't allowed yourself to grow and reach your full potential. This could be the case if your sole intent in getting an education, for example, was to land a job that would provide you with material possessions and security. You may have pushed yourself in some areas of growth but overlooked others. You may be denying the virtue and benefit of things that can enhance life.

Do you take risks?
How does it feel when you do?

What types of risks do you take in life? Are you willing to take risks that will make you feel uncomfortable? Write them down. Until you stretch past your comfort zone, you will not accelerate your growth. Many runners, for example, settle into a comfortable running pace even though they are capable of much more. I teach racers that they must push past this barrier if they are to excel.

Do you play it safe?

At work, do you let your boss hear only what he or she wants to hear? Do you underactualize your potential so that no one feels threatened by your intelligence? Are you intimidated by authority or worried about acceptance from your peers? Make a list of the ways in which you play it safe. Think about how you feel in those situations. It is especially important that you examine any long-held beliefs that are making your life so safe and secure that you do not develop to the next level. Don't be overprotective of yourself.

How do you control your emotions?

You may restrain your emotions in a variety of ways. List them. For example, you may overeat, overexercise, drink, take drugs, sleep too much or get sick frequently. You also may deny your own emotions, or you may take responsibility for everyone else's so that you have no time for your own.

Do you recognize the cause-and-effect relationship in your actions?

When communicating with others, beware of the tendency to say things just to stimulate a certain reaction. If you argue with someone, recognize that what you say will cause the other person to react. Do you see how his or her reaction might have been different had you acted differently? In the same way, do you provoke your partner in order to stir things up?

You must learn to control your emotions before you speak and express yourself in a non-blaming way. Learn self-control by asking yourself what the likely results of your words or actions will be. Begin to anticipate what could happen, positively or negatively. If you can speak reasonably and rationally, that's great. But that is often difficult when you are upset.

On the other hand, don't avoid talking to another person because you can't be entirely logical and clear about your emotions. People often rationalize a decision not to communicate by telling themselves that their reactions are not reasonable. So what? Just avoid blaming others and be clear about what bothers you. The other person will give you another perspective. If you are being irrational, then you can get back to what it is in your life that made you so sensitive to begin with. Unreasonable reactions are clues to areas you need to work on.

Do your motivations derive from fear?

Reacting from fear is a dangerous way to live. When you make changes in your life, your motivation should be something other than fear. You can create change just for the joy of it. You can take action from a positive, not a negative, stance.

119

Change is inevitable. It's our attitude toward it that makes all the difference. Once we accept that life is a process of change, we can be more positive about the events around us.

Make a list of the things you do, or don't do, which are motivated by fear. What would you like to change in your life? What is stopping you? Which changes do you accept and which do you not accept? Why do you resist change?

Are your expectations of others realistic?

When someone enters your life, ask yourself these simple questions: Why is this person here? What can we share? You must accept people for who they are, not for what you expect to come of the relationship. Identify what you really want from a relationship and see if the other person can fulfill those needs. By the same token, can you fulfill theirs? Is there a mutual basis for growth? Explain who you are, what you want and what you can give. Be honest about your real needs from the start and listen carefully to theirs. Don't waste your energy on counter-productive relationships.

How do you handle daily stress?

When you feel stressed and irritable, examine events of the day to identify any unresolved issues. At what moment did your irritability start? Never dismiss any thought or feeling as irrational. It may be—but it may also have some personal significance to you. Look at any ongoing factors or attitudes that contribute to your stress. Sometimes you need to resolve psychological problems before the physical manifestations go away and your balance is restored.

The connection between mental and physical pain can express itself in many ways. If your back feels tight and sore, for example, you may sit down to work but feel overburdened by your responsibilities. You may appear calm on the outside but feel quite anxious on the inside. Your job appears to be more than you can handle and you begin to feel incompetent. Your body processes these feelings as stress.

Are you bored with life?

When we are young, life seems to be full of new and exciting experiences. But as we age, we tend to establish well-worn patterns in our daily lives. Life becomes comfortable and routine. You eat the same breakfast cereal every day, watch the same television programs and even get out of bed on the same side each morning. When life becomes too mundane, boredom sets in.

As an adult, you must fight this boredom and stretch beyond your comfort zone. Otherwise, you will never grow. Think of the things you do consistently that have come to bore you. What can you do to break those patterns?

Where are you growing?
Where do you need to grow?

Make a chart with two columns. On one side, list the areas in your life where you need to grow. On the other, list the areas where you have grown. For example, if you would like to read more often or start an exercise program, write down those goals in the "need to grow" column.

Put the chart in a prominent place to remind yourself of

121

these goals. Note any progress you make on the chart each day. By writing down your intentions and reading them to yourself daily, you will send a clear message to your subconscious that you are ready and willing to change. These simple lists can help keep you alive and vital.

Were you ever victimized? How did this affect you?

Make a list of the ways in which you have been victimized. Are these incidents controlling your life today? If so, you must learn to forgive and let go of the past. It's time to move on with your life. Don't be a perpetual victim.

Were you given negative messages as a child?

As a child, you probably believed whatever your parents told you because they were authority figures. Their messages, positive or negative, were accepted at face value. The question is, how have you dealt with the negative messages they conveyed to you? To sort through this issue, make a list of your parents' attitudes, noting whether they are positive or negative. Then go back and note which attitudes you have adopted as your own, both toward yourself and regarding your expectations about the world.

Until you evaluate these messages and discard the negatives ones, they will remain a guiding force in your life. You now have an adult mind and adult ego strength. You have the ability to tolerate pain that you could not understand or handle as a child. You also have the opportunity to make important changes in yourself, provided you can find the courage to ask the hard questions about your past and present. When you stop blocking your awareness of your past hurts and current fears, you will gradually become energized. Your pain and fear will be less each time you make contact with them.

Are your choices driven by fear or by confidence?

Most people's lives are driven by fear. They avoid many of the things they want to say and do—such as confront their boss, their mate, their friends and perhaps their children—for fear of the consequences. They don't want to lose their job or to feel alone and unloved.

You must put aside your fears and build your confidence instead. Then you will be able to assert yourself in any situation. However, be careful not to confuse arrogance with confidence. Arrogant people act out of a need to feel superior. They, too, are motivated by fear and insecurity. When you are truly confident, you will feel good about your actions.

Do you respect boundaries?

In a relationship, do you communicate your boundaries to the other person and, in turn, respect his or hers? A mutual respect of boundaries must exist in an honest, healthy relationship. When these boundaries are overstepped, the process will distract from your time, joy and ability to utilize your love of life. Establish boundaries that feel comfortable and healthy to you.

Are you trusting?

Do you accept a person's word until he or she proves otherwise, or do you immediately label certain types of people as untrustworthy? If you have had a bad experience with several men, for example, do you conclude that all men are untrustworthy? Or can you judge each one on his own merits? Examine your prejudices and work to eliminate them.

What are your addictions?

Addictive behaviors mask reality. They allow you to disguise the areas of your life that are not working. List your addictions and their possible causes. You must identify the unfulfilled areas of your life that you have replaced with addictive behaviors and confront each one. Any behavior that you perform compulsively can be likened to an addiction in the sense that you use it to avoid feelings and maintain the illusion of control. You may eat, drink, work, fantasize or seek relationships in an addictive fashion.

Do you avoid responsibilities for fear of failure?

Our society measures success by what we have accomplished. We are deemed to be failures if we attempt something new and fail. This concept is reinforced when others praise us for our successes and reprimand us for our failures. We do not receive credit for having tried; rather, we are considered to be inadequate because we did not succeed.

A fear of failure prevents many people from taking on new

responsibilities that would allow them to grow. In reality, however, most successes are preceded by many failures. Go back in your life and assess your own failures. What did you learn from these experiences? Acknowledge yourself for having tried and for the lessons learned.

Are you looking to the right people for support?

You must share your dreams and goals with people who offer positive support. Some people will always find a hole in your plans, yet you may return to these unsupportive people time and again for support. Since their advice will only discourage you, be more aware of who you turn to for help. Watch your patterns and learn to interact with people who will be the most supportive and understanding of your needs and goals.

Are you a motivator or an instigator?

As an adult, you should be able to express yourself to friends without imposing your beliefs on them. Consider your communications: Do you say things that will enhance their lives? Are you insensitive to their feelings? If you respect other people's uniqueness, you will be sensitive in your approach to relating. Remember that what's important to you may not be important to them. Ask yourself, "Am I imposing my beliefs on this person? How would it feel to be on the receiving end of what I am sharing now?" If it doesn't feel right, then don't share it, at least not in that manner.

Are you on the road to burnout?

A variety of negative behavior patterns can lead to burnout, including compulsions, addictions, co-dependency, over-intensity and a tendency to go beyond your limits. The baby-boomer generation is an example. Their compulsive need to become highly educated and make money has caused them to burn out at an alarming rate.

You can prevent burnout by taking time to relax and have fun. The child within—an integral part of your nature—will guide you in this area. Don't be concerned that others may perceive you to be childlike. Expressing this part of yourself will keep you sane and prevent you from burning out.

Does self-doubt interfere with your life?

Many people undervalue themselves. They don't attach any value to their courage, intellect, creativity and other strengths. This mistaken perception can lead to self-doubt, as can poor reinforcement during your formative years. As a child, you may have been told that who and what you were was not good enough. But as an adult, you can recognize that you are more capable and lovable then you were led to believe. You can then replace self-doubt with self-confidence.

Do you try to force a relationship?

People who have not been valued for themselves often try to force a bond with others. In many cases, they control their relationships by using whatever approach worked in their families of origin. They may act weak and helpless so that others

126

feel responsible for them. They may use complaints and intimidation to gain control. Either way, they may believe they are strengthening the relationship when, in fact, they are undermining it. True bonds cannot be forced. They result when two people share and grow together.

Do you have hidden agendas?

When forming a relationship, be sure to explore and identify your motivations for doing so. It's best to communicate these motivations from the start, because they will eventually surface anyway and undermine the relationship. For example, you may discover that one hidden agenda in a relationship is financial security. If both partners do not know this, the relationship is bound to fail.

Does your life mimic your experiences or reflect the real you?

Along with negative cultural forces, early conditioning is the most common source of people's current life difficulties. Negative experiences will limit your life if you allow them to do so. You must become conscious of what has happened to you; otherwise, your life energy will be drawn to the same conditioned patterns until they are resolved. This repetition can make you feel limited, mistrusting, cynical or insecure. And it can keep you from reaching your full potential.

Consider this example: As a child, you became an extremely organized caretaker of others. Now, as a grown woman, you have no sense of your own needs because you are constantly trying to anticipate the needs of others and make things right for everyone around you. You have become overly active, controlling and detail oriented—all attitudes that cut you off from your intuition. To grow and reconnect to your feminine side, you must look at the past experiences that have limited you.

Do you react from reality or from conditioning?

Like most people, you probably express yourself based upon past experiences, rather than by reasoning through each situation in which you find yourself. If you assume that a person who is shabbily dressed must be poor and uneducated, for example, your reaction is based upon conditioned beliefs.

In the same way, you may allow feelings from previous situations to influence the present. Suppose that you lose a job and then take it out on your family. You are reacting from pent-up emotions, not from the reality of the moment. And your children, of course, will not understand your behavior. They may believe you are angry with them because they are bad. This can cause them to be confused in their relationships later on.

You need to examine your feelings and resolve them as they occur. Ask yourself if your emotions are related to the moment or if you are processing something from the past.

What energizes you?

Most people live passively. They expect the world and worldly things to entertain and excite them. Eventually, they lose touch with spontaneous emotion and rely on recycled energy from outside sources. They turn on the television set and watch the same unfunny shows, reacting along with the canned laughter. And they require extreme intensity to feel anything.

Hence, suspense movies have been replaced with grotesque horror films.

Society, for the most part, has lost its desire to self-energize. To foster the process of growth, you must be excited by your own potential and the many things you can do. You need to start each day with the influence of your inner self, not the outer world. You might decide to read more, engage in a hobby or learn a new skill. Or you might decide to spend the morning exercising instead of watching television passively.

Take control of your life. Do something constructive and you will become perpetually energized. When you get in tune with your inner self, you become more vital because you are engaging in uplifting activities that have personal meaning to you.

Do you feel hopeful or hopeless about important issues in your life?

Make a list of the things you feel either hopeless or hopeful about. In your "hopeless" column, note the areas that make you feel consistently hopeless. You can never stick to a diet, for example, or you can't seem to stop smoking. These items can serve as a guide, revealing where you need to go deeper to understand why you have created these patterns. Consider what happened in your life to make you feel this way.

Evaluate your "hopeful" column in the same manner. No doubt you succeed at certain things and feel hopeful about them because you devote the necessary energy to them. If you devote the same type of energy to the items in your hopeless column, you can begin to turn them around.

Do you let your emotions flow freely, or do you keep up a front?

Don't let problems accumulate and gnaw away at you from the inside. Resolve them as they occur. If something is bothering you, no one benefits if you smile on the outside and feel angry on the inside. Keeping up a false front has a negative influence on the expression of your true feelings. Let people know how you feel.

Do you mimic the example set by your parents?

Are you your own person? Like many adults, you will reflect your parental examples by doing exactly as they did or by doing the exact opposite. Make a list of your personality traits and compare them to those of your parents. Then, think about whether your characteristics reflect your true self. For example, your mother may have been totally submissive to your father. As a reaction, you may became the mirror image of her or the exact opposite, whereas your true nature is actually somewhere in between. Check each trait and think of ways to modify the extremes.

How do the roles you play affect your life?

List the roles you play in life, such as mother, daughter, sister, wife, lover and businesswoman.

Notice how your behavior may change depending on the role. For example, you may be a single parent who fills the roles of mother, father and friend to your children. At work you assume a subordinate role, and with your friends and acquaintances, you are dominant with some and passive with others. It's important to see how these roles interchange and affect your feelings and behaviors.

How do you handle your thoughts and feelings when they go against the social norm?

You must learn to live by your true feelings. If you suppress your beliefs for fear of scorn and ridicule, you will not contribute to the process of social change. Many people feel compassion toward cruelty and injustice, for example, but a part of them is afraid to rock the boat. They remain silent because they do not want to threaten their economic or social position or their political survival. When this silence occurs in the majority, important issues may never reach the forefront.

Indeed, change is generally brought about by a small group of people who are willing to speak out while the majority stands by. The lesson: If we do not use our power, somebody else will use theirs. And in the end, we lose control of our own lives.

How do you react to rejection?

Most people deny that rejection affects them. They pretend that it doesn't matter, adopting a "who wants to belong to their club anyhow" attitude. The truth is, nobody likes to be rejected. Rejection is a form of alienation that makes you feel you do not count. When you begin to feel isolated in this way, get in touch with your feelings and address the issue there and then. Reinforce the fact that you do count.

What happens to your unresolved feelings?

Unless you face your feelings and conflicts, a part of your energy will be consumed by the process of resolving them. And this, in turn, prevents you from living fully in the present. You'll also expend a huge amount of energy when you avoid situations that make you feel vulnerable. As a result, you will feel listless and underenergized. Remember that your future is your past. You need to shift your focus from problems to solutions, using your ingenuity, creativity and originality.

What are the socially accepted behaviors for women?

Society tends to cast women as powerless, helpless and dependent. And we often behave in the way people expect us to behave, forgetting that we have a choice. The media and movies portray women as victims or helpless people who need a strong man to hold things together, for example. But does that mean you have to follow these narrowly defined roles? Think about the behaviors you exhibit that do not reflect the real you. These are the ones you need to eliminate from your life.

Do you overlook your needs and cater to others?

Virtually everything we do is tempered by other people's feelings. When we do what others expect of us, we get good feelings and acceptance in return. The problem is, the actions that please others may not fulfill your inner needs. You must create space in your life for the things that make you feel like a whole person. While other people, such as your husband, may object to your pursuit of personal goals, ultimately both of you will benefit from a truer and more open relationship.

It takes courage to actualize your needs. Identify the essential parts of yourself and the real needs that were ignored, denied or misunderstood when you were growing up. Recognize them now and begin to deal with them. You must discover who you are and what you want to do. Then you must take action. Taking the views of others into consideration is fine; allowing them to intimidate or control you is not.

Do you strive for love and acceptance or success?

Materialism does not necessarily have to negate love, but in our society it generally does. That's because so many people have sacrificed attention to self and others to achieve their goals. If you have sacrificed love for material success, think about what you can do to restore some balance in your life.

How do you define love?

Love is the manifestation of life. It radiates joy, comfort, kindness and patience. You're drawn to its energy. You know when love is being shared—and when it isn't—by listening to your heart. If someone falsely claims to love you, or tries to prove his love with material possessions, you know it's not real because you do not feel it. You may have lost your ability to love if you are impatient with yourself and others. You will become busy outwardly to compensate for the coldness and lack of love you feel inside.

True love is given freely, with no expectations attached. If you are filled with love, you give it automatically. If you require a response, you are motivated by the need for acceptance or another ulterior motive. Why do you think Mother Teresa does more to help disadvantaged people than all the hospitals and welfare centers put together? It's because she accepts people for who they are and passes no judgment. No matter that they are petty thieves, muggers, itinerant farmers or lepers. She doesn't say, "I can't love you because of your faults." She just loves.

Every human being is capable of being loving. But you will not know how to open the love inside you until someone has given love to you. Think of something or someone you love. Do you give that love unconditionally or do you expect something in return? Who are you really giving for? Be honest about your motives. It's important to understand why you do something. You need to feel good about what you do and recognize that love emanates from within.

Is your need for love fulfilled?

You've probably been conditioned to believe that you are undesirable until someone loves you. Parental and societal norms tell us that we will gain love by getting married, having a family and carrying on the traditions. This conditioning has caused most single people in our society to feel miserable. By these rules, love cannot exist outside a narrowly defined relationship. But what about a relationship with life, work and yourself? What about a relationship between friends? Most people overlook these valid expressions of love.

What is the difference between having something with love or without love?

Anything built from love is empowering because it derives from what is real. Conversely, anything created without love is disempowering and based on an illusion. Ultimately, it will collapse because illusions are held together by force. You may use illusions to force a relationship or fall prey to illusions in which others force their will on you.

In many cult movements, for example, the leaders will tell you that they alone love you. They may brainwash you to believe that your family should be feared instead of loved. Then when a family member calls, your heart pounds and you begin to sweat. Such incidents serve to reinforce the cult's power over you. But in time the illusion will dissipate and you will be back to nothing.

Love, on the other hand, empowers and strengthens us. If you love yourself and love life, diseases do not have the space to manifest. Make a list of the things you really love and those you are involved in that do not feel right to you. Do the same thing for the people in your life. With whom do you associate out of a genuine respect for that person? With whom do you feel uncomfortable? Do these people and situations give to you or take from you? Are they concerned for your well-being or for theirs alone?

Are you seeking love in the wrong way?

If the love you received as a child was conditional—based on your ability to please your parents—then as an adult you will seek love and acceptance through the same actions that gained you recognition in your early years. Perhaps you are an overzealous worker who stays late night after night, trying to please the boss and gain his recognition. In essence, you are reverting to the action-for-praise syndrome instilled by your parents. This tendency affects your well-being by restricting growth and reinforcing the feeling that you are not acting from your own center. Be careful what you do to gain love and acceptance. Evaluate the things you do out of a need to be loved and those you do out of joy. Do the same for the people in your life. Do you feel loved and accepted for who you are or for what you do?

What are your most blissful moments?

Each of us has a different concept of bliss. Depending on the person, bliss may be walking in the woods, watching a sunset or listening to rain on a roof. It's a feeling of perfect harmony that comes over us when we are in tune with nature. We do not feel threatened or imbalanced. List these moments and describe the role love played in them.

How do you deny love?

What are the ways that you avoid love? Perhaps you make love trivial, escape from it, fail to communicate it or find fault with people so as not to accept their love. Look for the subtle avoidance mechanisms, such as overeating, displacing anger or communicating dishonestly. Indeed, the most effective way to avoid love is to become involved in false and deceptive sharing.

What do you daydream and fantasize about?

Make a list of your recurring fantasies, including those that do not appear to fit into your life. These daydreams reflect your inner needs and should become an integral part of your life. If you're excited by the idea of a trip to New Mexico to study Native American crafts, don't dismiss it simply because you don't have the money or it seems impractical. By so doing, you deny expression to an important part of yourself called the creative child.

The daydreams that occupy your mind need to be explored. They are essential parts of your nature. Keep notes about your fantasies and daydreams. Evaluate each one as a need in your life. They can be a new beginning.

Are you filled with love or despair?

Love energizes us, while despair drains our energy. We must focus on love, not the negative force of despair, if we are to keep ourselves physically, mentally and emotionally charged. Both forces are potentially present at any given time. But we have choices about which emotion we will emphasize.

Are you afraid to express love?

Many people do not express love for fear of being rejected, misunderstood or taken advantage of. They may pretend to be independent and aloof. They may act as if they don't need anyone to feel complete when, in fact, they are craving love. Or they may suffer quietly. You never know how these people truly feel because they act as if everything is okay. They have never been allowed to express their feelings.

List some of the ways in which you disguise your feelings, especially your need for love. Work to resolve these.

Can you give and receive love if you are invulnerable?

You must be vulnerable to experience love. Like most people, however, you may try to be invulnerable because you expect the worst from people and fear getting hurt. As you age, you lose the ability to love others and feel their love. Perhaps you can't even feel love toward your children. You're too busy to spend time with them, but they don't understand why. In the process, you hurt them, hurt your relationship and perpetuate the pattern by teaching them to become invulnerable. They, too, may one day be incapable of experiencing love.

Look at your patterns of behavior toward others. Then look at the patterns in the people around you. You may see in others what you cannot see in yourself.

What limits your desire to love?

Your ability and desire to love may be limited by anger, fear, envy, resentment or hostility. The more of these emotions you feel—and the more intense the conditioning from which they derived—the more frustrated you will feel in your ability to love. This conditioning must be addressed and changed. Write yourself a new contract on life. Examine the conditioning that caused you to believe and react in certain ways. Write down what you need and want from life, and then go after it. Work on replacing conditioned beliefs with the things you truly want.

Do you suffer from love addiction?

Do you depend on someone else to make you feel good about yourself? Must others accept you before you can love yourself? If so, you may suffer from the love addiction that occurs in dysfunctional families and relationships. If you only feel good when someone gives you emotional strokes, you had better start concentrating on what's missing in your life. Think about the type of people to whom you are drawn. Note their positive qualities and develop these in yourself. By the same token, think about the negative attitudes that tend to attract you. See if you possess these attitudes toward yourself.

How do social norms and religious morals affect your ability to share love?

Organized religion has done more to suppress our natural desires and diminish true love than any other force in history. Religion has tremendous power to suppress love when it is separatist and laced with conditions and rules. Some religions tell us that we are not supposed to love people of other races, colors or religions. We learn to mistrust others and react negatively to them. They become the enemy.

On the positive side, religion can help you to understand your spiritual nature and the ethics and morals that should be common to all people. That makes religion a paradox; it may help you or suppress you, encourage you or deny you. Give some thought to your religion: what about it helps you to share love, and what causes you to suppress it?

Do you blame others for not being there for you?

Most children cannot express the anger they feel toward their parents for hurting or abandoning them. This is especially true of young children, who do not have the intellectual or physical capabilities to fend for themselves. Rather than speak up, they repress their feelings deep in their psyches. But these hurts will surface in distorted ways later in life. Often they are acted out in relationships, when you react to your partner as if he were a parent. You will blame others for the hurt caused by your parents, and others will blame you in the same way.

To have healthier, more constructive relationships, you need to address these issues as they arise. Learn to distinguish between the criticisms directed at you and those projected onto you. If you or your partner act as a substitute parent, then you must question whether the relationship is truly healthy.

Do you allow passion to enter your communications and experience?

You must be passionate about your life and dynamic in expressing your feelings. Passion gives you the momentum to go forward day after day, despite all the obstacles you encounter and the naysayers who want to limit your enjoyment and achievements. To actualize your passion—be it poetry, painting, dancing or medicine—you must be self-motivated.

Parents often encourage children to manifest an energy level that matches their own. They may express these restrictions openly with statements such as, "Calm down. There's nothing to get so excited about," or "Put on a happy face. You should be happy." Perhaps they are more subtle and simply do not respond when you express energies that are markedly different from theirs.

Compare your passions to the fears that have motivated and directed your life. What actions have you taken in life due to a fear of not being accepted, loved and secure? By removing those false security guides, you can manifest the passion that will take you the rest of the way.

What are your innermost expectations?

At every stage of your life, you must have certain expectations for yourself. If you don't, you will stop growing, and the dynamic forward motion of life will come to a halt. What's more, you should have the passion to implement these expectations. List your expectations and then decide whether or not you can and will actualize them.

How do you validate your self-esteem inwardly and outwardly?

When you feel good about who you are, no matter what you are doing, you validate your sense of self. And when you feel good about yourself, even in the face of failure, you raise your self-esteem. Many women suffer a damaged sense of self-esteem when their relationships stop working. They feel depressed, but may only display their emotions through anger or tears to someone with whom they feel comfortable.

Think of a goal or event in your life that did not work out. Did you feel good about yourself despite the failure, or did you consider yourself less worthy because of it? Most important, can you continue to pursue your dreams despite the risk of failure, or do you let it stop you?

Do you try to get others to validate your self-worth?

Do you acknowledge people intellectually, or even try to please them, when you disagree with them or know they are wrong? While this tactic will gain you acceptance, it may very well cost you your self-respect. Making people feel good at your expense is not healthy. Only honest acknowledgement is.

In some cases, you may try to gain others' approval by allowing them to transgress your boundaries. You may allow them to enter any part of your life, at any time, for any reason. In the process, you will lose your sense of autonomy and subjugate yourself to the other person. This is especially true of women.

Note the things you do to please others even though these actions feel wrong to you. Evaluate your reasons for submitting to others. What would happen if you were to be yourself and honestly express how you feel? In what areas do you need to be more assertive? What steps can you take in that direction?

If you told the truth about your real inner needs, how would the people in your life view you?

Don't be afraid to communicate your real feelings and needs. You'll never go forward unless you have the courage to express them. Indeed, many people go through life wondering "What would have happened if . . . ?" They are more concerned with how others will react and respond to hearing their needs than they are with having those needs met.

Think of what you would say to your boss or coworkers about your real needs. What would you say to your friends, family and lover? If a person cannot accept you because you communicate your needs, can you fulfill your needs in spite of that?

How do you relate to others, positively and negatively?

Pay attention to the effect you have on other people. How do they respond when you relate to them? You may discover that you are often too busy to listen to your children, or that you ignore certain people in the same way that others ignore you. Think about your reaction when other people do not know how to communicate with you. Do you try to find out more about them, or do you simply dismiss them as having nothing of interest to say because they are quiet? Some people have a difficult time communicating, but their silence does not mean they do not have feelings. Are you able to extend yourself to help another open up?

Do you allow yourself to be used by others?

Sometimes we blame others for using us, when in reality we have set ourselves up to be used. This is a co-dependent pattern of behavior—the need to be needed. Then we feel anger, guilt, depression, the need to eat compulsively or some other displaced energy, all stemming from a negative situation we have created ourselves. Pay attention to your patterns of behavior, and analyze the circumstances when you feel you have been used.

Do you see the larger context of smaller actions?

Your viewpoint will become too narrow in scope if you do not recognize the bigger picture of your everyday actions. Suppose that you work in a munitions factory. Can you see that your work ultimately will be used for destruction, or do you consider yourself to be separate and removed from the product's purpose?

In which areas of life do you feel incompetent?

People commonly feel incompetent in the areas of life they have avoided. But you must pay attention to these areas and challenge yourself to become more proficient. Determine which areas are difficult for you now. How can you address them?

Do you overreact?

Overreaction usually stems from insecurity. It is a defense mechanism that keeps you from going forward in an uncomfortable situation. By overreacting, you focus on the reaction itself rather than on a realistic plan to confront a problem and make constructive change. Consider this example: You know you need to eat better, but you sabotage yourself by saying, "Health food is too expensive. What's the point of eating healthy if I don't have the time or money to do it right?" Most of the time what you imagine is far worse than reality. You've overreacted.

Beyond that, you may overreact to minor things other people say or do. Instead of reasoning with them, you go into a rage and lash out at the person. If someone you are with wants to go to a particular restaurant, and you don't, you may become angry instead of talking rationally about the event. You believe that the only way for you to be heard is to scream. Needless to say, this can damage a relationship irreparably. It is far better to reason through a problem.

To make constructive changes in your life and maintain healthy relationships, it is important for your thoughts and behaviors to be appropriate. List the instances in your life when you have overreacted. Beware of these inappropriate thoughts as they arise and resolve to be more reasonable than reactive.

Do you acquiesce to authority?

Think back to your childhood. Did your parents or guardians only demonstrate affection when you were completely submissive to them? If so, you grew up believing that you must please those in positions of authority to gain their acceptance. Now, you might take the same approach to pleasing your boss or other authority figures. Perhaps you rush to get coffee for the boss, or you grin and bear it when you work late most every night. You think you must please people; they can't just like you for yourself.

Acquiescing to others does not make people like you more. To the contrary, it gives them the impression that you are weak, helpless and insecure. And it gives them more of an opportunity to take advantage of you. List the ways in which you acquiesce to authority to gain acceptance.

Do you take statements out of context to justify your feelings?

People often hear only what they want to, not what is actually being said. They twist others' statements to justify their beliefs. If a friend tells you she was mugged by a black man and you conclude that all minority people are dangerous, you have used what she told you to justify your own beliefs. This way of thinking can keep you locked in your fears.

Do your belief systems limit you?

You can become stuck in ineffectual behavior patterns when you react out of habit. Rather than examine your life and initiate the process of change, you choose to recycle the same old doubts and fears. A homemaker who feels frustrated by this role, for example, may allow her belief system to prevent her from pursuing other avenues in life. She may feel that she is capable only of being a housekeeper, wife and mother.

If you follow the behavior patterns to which you are accustomed, you will continue to have the same doubts about your abilities and will remain frustrated that your needs are not being met. If, however, you expand your world and look toward other women who are overcoming similar obstacles, you will get the support and direction you need to change.

List the habitual types of behavior that keep you feeling trapped and frustrated. Think of new ways to deal with your problems. Look to role models and support systems outside of yourself for help in forming new paradigms.

Do you respond to all relationships in the same way?

You need to be adaptable in your relationships. Recognize that each relationship is unique. You may be able to share cultural interests with one friend, engage in sports with another and find a spiritual soulmate in a third. Note where you are rigid in your relations with others. Ask yourself, "What is unique about this person that can enhance my life?"

Do you avoid change because of the accompanying pain and anxiety?

Change is not a pain-free process, but that doesn't mean you should avoid it. If you want to correct a deformity in your back caused by poor posture, you will have to experience pain as you begin to straighten up. Sometimes the anxiety you feel when anticipating change is worse than the experience itself. If you fear the dentist, for instance, you may postpone taking care of

147

your teeth. But once the dental work is done, you are happy you went.

You will feel anxiety and pain any time you let go of the predictable, such as an old job or a long-term relationship. A conflict arises because you are afraid to let go of what's familiar, even though you know that you must move on. To grow, you must work through the pain of relinquishing the attitudes, relationships and beliefs that no longer work for you.

Life is constant motion and change. To deny that reality and cling to the familiar is impossible; this approach will bring unhappiness and pain in the long run. Letting go, on the other hand, may be painful at first. But ultimately it will free you.

Do you let other people define who you are?

Try not to see yourself through the eyes of others. You will give up your identity, autonomy and integrity by engaging in such co-dependent behavior. Another person can never know you as you know yourself and can never experience what you have experienced. Therefore, you may seriously shortchange yourself when you let another person define who you are.

Make a list of the qualities that define you. Look in the mirror and affirm who you are.

Are you addicted to your relationship?

If you experience terrible anxiety and fear at the very thought of losing your relationship, you are addicted to it and co-dependent. You may even believe that you cannot live without the relationship. As a result, you do everything possible to maintain your involvement, even if that means compromising your integrity, honesty, pleasure and growth. Your relationship becomes the antithesis of what it ought to be.

Now is the time to make a conscious effort to do things that are good for you. Focus on goals and experiences that add meaning to your life. Also, seek outside support to help you overcome your co-dependency.

Issues of Interest to Men

And The Masculine Side Of Women

> *Happy men have a passion for life; they express themselves openly and with vitality. They are content with their lives.*

7

Do you hold back your feelings?

In our culture, the typical male upbringing generally dictates that we not show our emotions. For the most part, men are encouraged to be active, to achieve and to perform great feats. Any feelings that distract from performance are to be suppressed. Our society's undervaluation of the feeling function (if we let them, feelings function as a form of intelligence) has contributed paradoxically to an underproductive, underenergized workforce and to joyless relationships with others. We cut off our feelings at a steep price.

People use various defense mechanisms to cut off their feelings. Addictive behavior is a common defense mechanism and a potentially dangerous one. An addictive behavior can be anything that you do repetitively to avoid deeper pain. Do you run from your feelings by overworking? Overeating? Buying things you don't need? Spending hours in front of the television set? With any such addiction, you will feel that you do not have complete freedom of choice about performing the behavior. You will feel emotionally attached to it.

If this description rings true for you, now is the time to eliminate the addictive behavior from your life. By doing so, you will be able to grow and achieve real stability and peace. Any feelings that you avoid will always return until you deal with them. By running away from reality, you lose any opportunity to gain insight into yourself, and you do not treat yourself with respect. You may cause severe physical harm to yourself if your addiction involves the abuse of chemicals or foods, for example, and you may cause harm to those around you if negative emotions erupt explosively. You are not in control of your constructive energy.

To achieve balance, you must become familiar with your emotional life. Spending an hour each day writing in your journal will be of great help to you. Your writing will make you aware of what is working negatively in your life, and you will learn how to make changes that promote growth and happiness. You should set aside a specific time each day for this activity. Be sure to write in your journal when you feel yourself in the grip of a negative emotion. If your journal is not at hand, jot down a note to help you later recall what prompted the negative mood.

The very act of stopping to write about a feeling, rather than suppressing it, will help you break your usual negative patterns of coping. Never dismiss any thought, visual image or feeling that comes to mind when you are writing. To do so would only lead you to another defense mechanism—the tendency to minimize the importance of your feelings by saying they are stupid or of no consequence.

What do you want from your work?

If you're like most men, you tend to derive a large part of your identity and sense of self-worth from your work. Your job is a top priority, and it may take precedence over other aspects of your life. But have you considered what your motivations are in making work so important? And have you considered whether or not your current work truly fulfills your needs? For example, you may expect your job to meet your needs for the following:

- Identity
- Friendship
- Growth

Identity

Your performance at work affects the deeper meaning of your life. If you do well in your business or on the job, you feel good about yourself. There's a certain pride that comes from knowing you did a good job. You get positive feedback from others around you.

Friendship

The work environment promotes natural associations that can form into friendships. Some friendships stay in the workplace, while others carry over into your personal life. It's easy to see why such bonds are created at work. Not only do you have a lot in common with the people there, but you also see them on a daily basis.

Growth

Does your work honor your values? Or must you compromise your beliefs or feelings to conform to your workplace? For example, if your co-workers smoke and you are afraid it will affect your health, do you suffer in silence or are you willing to ask your boss to change the situation? If he won't, would you quit your job and look for a workplace that does not compromise your health?

If you must compromise your beliefs to maintain a job, eventually your whole life will be adversely affected. You'll stop caring about your work and yourself as well. Your work may become sloppy, or you may start to feel miserable and take it out on others. When you can't control your environment, you will feel out of control in all other areas of your life.

The lesson: You must evaluate your work honestly to determine if it respects your real needs. Ask yourself, does my job help me to grow intellectually, emotionally, socially and spiritually? If your work is personally meaningful, you will be much happier and healthier for it.

What do you want from your home life?

Make a note of the things you have been taught to want from your home life and the things you really want. If you experience intense feelings that you do not understand or cannot be flexible in certain respects, your conditioned (or learned) needs may be ruling your life. Some of these areas include:

- Dominance
- Hero identity
- Spiritual renewal

Dominance

Does your conditioning make you feel that you must be the dominant member of your family? Must the final decision always be yours? Are you afraid of competition from your wife and other family members? If so, you must recognize that these are conditioned responses. More important, they are far from conducive to a healthy family life. If you don't respect the abilities of others and allow everyone in your family an equal right of expression, you can expect deterioration in those relationships.

Hero identity

Do you expect unconditional hero worship from your family members, or do you earn their respect and admiration? Give some thought to the actions you take, on a regular basis, to make your family look up to you.

Spiritual renewal

Do you gain a sense of spiritual renewal from your home life? Does it revitalize you from the pressures of the outside world? You can use your home life to practice and reaffirm connection to others at a feeling and intuitive level.

You need to honor the peace and space of your home. It is unfair to you and your family to bring problems home from work. Be aware that you may be talking excessively and brooding about your job to avoid intimacy. So leave your problems at work, except for a short talk about the day's events that allows both you and your mate to put the day's problems behind you.

Is your life what you really want it to be?

List the important areas of your life. These may include work, friendships, family, location, lifestyle and anything else that comes to mind. Note what works and what doesn't in each area. List your dreams and aspirations for each. Do you view your goals with pleasure, or do they reflect what you think you ought to want?

Begin to separate your real needs from those that are merely superficial. For example, if you enjoy wide open spaces, perhaps you shouldn't be living in the city. That doesn't mean you must move immediately, but this knowledge certainly can be factored into your long-term planning. You may have to consider practical matters such as job availability and school quality, but the time you spend researching the possibilities will stimulate your ability to transform your life.

You must learn to follow your heart. You may think of a long list of excuses to avoid making changes in your life— career responsibilities, family, lack of education—but these excuses ultimately prevent you from reaching your full potential. Allow yourself to trust your own perceptions.

What are your heroic qualities?

Everyone possesses certain heroic qualities or has certain heroic images to which they aspire. List yours. Perhaps you are capable of compassion, introspection, endurance, persistence, discipline, strength or courage. Do you manifest these qualities? If so, in what areas of your life?

Unless you examine your heroic qualities, you may overlook them. And this oversight could deny you a viable route to personal growth. Your heroic images help to motivate you. They serve as a catalyst for change that allows you to overcome your fears and move forward with your life.

Do you define your own life?

You must define your life by the needs and beliefs that are important to you, not by the standards of other people. Many people are a product of their upbringing, cultural heritage, peer pressures and other people's expectations.

The process of reevaluating your needs and redefining your life is ongoing. If you don't like yourself, perhaps you are not acknowledging your true needs and living honestly. Instead, you are living out the stereotypes dictated by your earlier conditioning. If you do like yourself, then you will be comfortable enough to change the things that need to be changed. You must create an identity that fulfills your needs and desires and then make the dynamic changes necessary to live this life. Remember the heroic qualities you have just listed in establishing your identity.

What are your successes and failures?

Acknowledge your successes and learn from your failures. It's important not to berate yourself when you fail at a new endeavor. Instead, look at the ways in which you have grown from the experience. You've probably grown in ways you do not even appreciate. Recognize how your difficulties have strengthened you and acknowledge the new experiences you've allowed yourself to have. Don't dismiss these lessons in life.

Men tend to be too hard on themselves. They don't give

themselves enough credit for the life experiences they have survived. Make a list of events in your life that have required you to confront major survival issues, such as the death of a parent, the loss of a job or the breakup of a relationship. Take an honest, careful look at the hardships you have been through. What lessons did you learn? Don't underevaluate yourself and your ability to respond to such crises.

Recognize your victories as well. You don't have to be a braggart and exaggerate the significance of your achievements, but you should enjoy your successes before letting them go. Too many people discount their accomplishments and thus deprive themselves of a well-deserved boost to their self-esteem.

Do you follow your intuition?

Do you trust your own intuitive abilities, or do you feel you must be in control at all times to make your life work? It is often difficult to trust our intuitive function if we had early problems with bonding. Without a secure attachment to a protecting parent, the frightened child creates a false ego which may appear to others to be very strong. The child is pretending to himself and to the world. He reacts in whatever way he believes is necessary for survival. He may be compliant, aggressive, adorable—whatever will cause others to respond and attend to his needs. But the ego is not acting out of its own center; it is reacting rigidly out of fear. The frightened ego is threatened by the spontaneous feelings of our intuitive function (including spontaneous images, thoughts and body sensations). Spontaneity and feeling are frightening to the child who has learned to cut off his pain.

To recover our intuitive abilities, we must learn to recognize when we are being phony (that's our frightened false ego at work) and little by little to become more genuine. We must look behind the front we have created and eventually allow our selves to welcome all feelings, both positive and negative, because they will provide important guidance in life. They will allow you an understanding of yourself and others that cannot be achieved by rational thought alone. You will learn when to trust and when not to trust. You'll know when to say no. You will learn to set comfortable limits at work and at home.

Can you recall a time in your life when you did not follow your intuition? What did the experience teach you? Based on that experience and others, can you now allow your intuition to influence your thoughts?

If you were to die today, what legacy would you leave?

Make a list of the accomplishments and qualities for which you will be remembered. Is your legacy a positive or negative one? Are you leaving something for others or taking only for yourself? What have you created that's unique? Where have you taken a chance? If you take no risks in life, you can manifest no legacy.

Do you associate with negative people?

List the people with whom you associate. Are they a positive or negative influence? Some people manage to see the bad in everything. When you're around them, their negativity will rub off on you. As much as possible, disassociate yourself from the people who have a negative influence on your life. Instead, choose to associate with people who are positive and supportive of your ideas, your spontaneity and your honesty.

Are you able to say no?

Make a list of the times you said no—or wish you had—to acting in ways that betray your true self. How many times would you have prevented a problem had you done so? When you have the courage to say no, you take back the power to be who you are.

Are you able to make commitments? Do you make too many?

Do you have a tendency to make more commitments than you can uphold? Analyze a typical month of your life to determine your patterns of making and keeping commitments. Be alert to the possibility that you leave no time for yourself.

Are you a workaholic?

Work should not be all important in your life, to the exclusion of all other interests. In our society, however, some men work so hard they forget how to relax. They even work around the house during their vacations. If you fit this workaholic pattern, you must begin to develop other aspects of your life. Let in other influences besides the work ethic. Otherwise, you may very well end up with ulcers, high blood pressure and other diseases as a result of the constant pressure.

Evaluate the time you spend working and the time you spend

pursuing other interests. See if this division is in balance. If you work so hard that you haven't developed other parts of your life, you need to take time out for yourself. Only then can you do the things necessary for personal growth. Make a list of the nonwork activities you might enjoy, and commit to doing one each week. If you are unsuccessful in taking time off, picture yourself enjoying a pleasurable activity. Note your thoughts and feelings about taking that time for yourself. Do you feel guilty? Out of control? Gratified? What else? Write down how you think others will react if you take time for yourself. The reactions you imagine are probably your attitudes toward yourself. Try checking them out with people close to you.

Do you communicate honestly?

Make a list of your real needs. Do you let people know what these needs are, or do you mask them? Can you let another person know that he or she has hurt your feelings? One way you might do this is to say, "Right now I don't feel good about what you said." If you choose to say nothing, it will only build up as resentment. Think of how many times you have let an incident go by and then replayed the scenario over and over in your mind. All sorts of possible responses come to mind after the fact, but it's too late because you have not communicated honestly. Conversely, are you able to express positive feelings to others? You cannot control the past, but you certainly can learn from it. More importantly, you can resolve to express your feelings honestly when similar situations arise in the future.

How attentive are you to your personal needs?

If you don't pay attention to your own needs, who will? No one else really knows you. They only know the aspects of yourself that you are willing to share. Meanwhile, part of what you share is your conditioned self, not the real you.

You need to get in touch with your real needs. These may include a need for nurturing, love, expression, compassion, humility and openness. Define your needs and determine what you are willing to do to obtain them. How many of these non-working parts of yourself are you willing to let go so that you can replace the old with the new?

Make lists of your real needs and your conditioned needs. Decide which ones you want to get rid of and which you would like to place more emphasis on.

Do you take time out to nurture your growth?

Personal growth comes from the learning process. But how many of us devote time each day to learning experiences? To check your progress in this area, make a list of the things you do to enhance your growth.

Like many people, you may believe there is a point at which learning stops. For example, you may think you have reached your full potential—and therefore can no longer grow—once you receive an education, master a career or have a family. But this is not the case, of course. We all need to learn and develop in certain areas throughout our lives. You may need to learn better communication skills or more patience, for example. Or you may want to master a craft or to learn more about life. In

163

any event, the things you want to know more about can enhance your life and make it more meaningful.

Are you willing to take a chance?

Most men look for a secure outcome—a sure thing—before they venture into unknown areas. But this approach limits them from trying new things, since it is impossible to know the outcome of unfamiliar actions. As you approach the top of a hill, you never know what you will find on the other side. When you move or get a new job, you don't know what changes that action will put into motion. You need self-confidence to enjoy the process of change. Don't put limits on your life just because you can't control the outcome.

Are you aware of your power and control? How do you use them?

No doubt you feel that you have control over some areas of your life, but not over others. You may have power at work and not at home, or vice versa. You must gain control of the parts of your life in which you wish to grow. The process of becoming self-aware will give you that control. Do not criticize yourself for feeling anxious or uncertain about this process. Instead, consider such feelings to be indicators that you have some work to do in that area. Never reject or avoid your feelings by engaging in substitute behaviors.

Finally, make a list of the areas in your life where you have control and the ways in which you use that power. Do you use it in a positive way to nurture relationships and aid other people? Or do you use it in a negative way to control others? Do you use control to make your life work in a more spontaneous way? Or do you use it to maintain the status quo?

There are two basic types of men: Those who are in control of their lives and those who are not. The first group uses their control in a constructive way. Being in control gives them a sense of power, but they do not abuse it. Rather, they use self-empowerment to create more and better options for living. They look at alternative solutions to their problems and choose the ones that are most feasible.

In the second group the men are angry about their lack of control. They emote a quiet suffering, a martyrdom. These people are likely candidates for illnesses such as ulcers, heart disease, constipation, obesity and addictive behaviors.

Do you compromise your beliefs in order to feel secure?

List the ways in which you compromise your principles. Do you act meek on the job? Do you try to mask your insecurity by acting righteous at church or staunch and tough at home? If so, you must begin to face your fears and free your energy.

You may compromise your creativity for the security of a job you hate, for example, by reasoning that jobs are scarce and that you could never survive at the work you truly enjoy. That isn't true. Open your mind and change your values and beliefs so that you can pursue the interests that make you feel most comfortable. If your religious and educational upbringing has conditioned you to believe that your capabilities are limited, then you must overcome this conditioning before you can grow.

Look over your list of principles and decide which ones have

How do you deal with conflict?

true relevan
principles in

Most peo
cause they
don't want
don't have
him to be
anything wi
ple than fac

Hero-wo
times. Whe
about myth
Rocky. In f
who overca

You nee
than projec
Write dow
how many
to develop
but some p

Imagine
and vulner
this spectr
and feeling

You may deal with conflict in one of three ways: by being dynamic and meeting the situation head-on to resolve it immediately; by complying externally while denying your true feelings (saying yes when you mean no); or by glossing over the problem as if it did not exist.

Of these three, only the dynamic method allows you to get problems out of the way and move on to other things. Make a list of all the unresolved problems in your life. Try to think of a dynamic way to resolve each one.

How has your childhood conditioning of right and wrong affected your life?

The training you receive as a child directly affects your concept of right and wrong and your self-concept as a man, including your notions about whether or not feelings may be expressed. This training will determine whether you feel disempowered or empowered in life, dominating or cooperative and spontaneous.

The rules from your childhood may cause you to react unrealistically to present situations. If your pet died when you were a child, for example, your parents may have told you that you had to be a big boy and not cry. In that case, you may not be able to cry as an adult. When we are rejected and we do not deal with the rejection, it will continue to manifest later in our lives. The only difference now is that we will have chosen socially acceptable ways of displaying rejection.

Examine the following list of feelings and check the ones you might still be carrying from childhood. If you are unsure, try picturing yourself in a scene (at home, at work or during childhood) in which the feeling or attitude is being expressed:

helplessness	bravery
grief	calmness
domination	capability
defeat	inspiration
cheating	security
betrayal	helpfulness
abandonment	freedom
shame	gratification
fright	energy
being discounted	childishness
emptiness	contentment
envy	kindness
hate	mysticism
intimidation	poetry
loneliness	peace
persecution	relaxation
obsession	sexuality
rejection	tenderness
temptation	valor
vulnerability	wonderment
affection	heroism
bliss	selflessness

I have listed these categories because they are the ones that affect my life. You may have different emotions and feelings that need to be considered. The important point is that each one must be examined to determine if any remaining conflicts need to be resolved. Once a resolution is reached, you can free up your personality to be who you really are. You will not be limited by your conditioning.

What are your excesses and what motivates them?

When you feel discontented and angry—when things aren't going your way—you may tend to overindulge. You may overeat, overwork, chain smoke or overindulge in sex, drugs or alcohol. Some people try to resolve these symptoms without addressing the cause. If you overeat because you are not content, for example, you cannot resolve the problem by trying to lose weight. You must get to the root of the problem, your sense of discontent.

To begin this process, make a note each time you experience these negative emotions and each time you overindulge. Eventually, you may see a connection between the two. Everything has a cause and effect. Once you make the connection, it will be easier for you to resolve the underlying problems and eliminate any related excessive behavior.

When do you feel content?

Learn to recognize the times in your life when you feel a sense of satisfaction—the times when everything feels right. Make a note of the events that transpired and caused this feeling, and then encourage yourself to linger in the moment. Too many men are almost afraid to feel good about their lives. If you always feel unappreciated by the people around you, it may be that you have lost the capacity to accept positive feelings from others. Perhaps you believe you don't deserve them. As a result, you may retreat to the comfort of the familiar—no matter how painful that reaction may be—and minimize the appreciation of others. You may not even hear their positive feedback.

Equally important, beware of the times when you feel good one moment and then terrible the next. That's withdrawal. It shows that you are not connected to your feelings. You don't accept yourself, and you're never satisfied with your accomplishments. This dissatisfaction forces you on to the next project and the same short-lived sense of accomplishment. You are acting out of a lack of self-esteem, rather than a genuine sense of achievement and the spirit of congratulation. Take the time and effort to recreate your good feelings whenever possible. Men tend to overlook these feelings. In the process, they miss out on one of the great joys of life.

What things do you value in life?

Do you value your family, friends and work? If so, how do you measure their value? Value is what you get from participating in the relationship, whether it be nurturing, love or friendship. If you do not have a sense of value, you will tend to take things for granted. You may have a wonderful person in your life, for example, but fail to fully appreciate the benefits received from the relationship.

Make a list of the people in your life and their value to you. Do you make them aware of their true value? By communicating their importance to you, you make it much easier for them to reciprocate. That means the relationship will be nurtured so that both of you may grow.

Do you value yourself?

List the things you like about yourself. Above all, you need
to be happy with yourself. And you need to understand that
nobody is perfect. If you tend to be your own worst critic, begin
to allow yourself some room to be human.

Did you gain acceptance from your parents?

If you are like most men, you did not bond well with your
father as a child. Our society dictates that a child's initial bonding will be with his mother, from the time of birth well into
childhood. At some point, your father is expected to bond with
you intellectually and nurture your abilities, while showing love
and understanding when you fail.

But many fathers tend to be judgmental when showing their
appreciation for a task well done. The reason is that a father
wants his son to be a better man than he is. This approach will
deliver the false message that your father is more interested in
the results of your abilities than in a true loving relationship.
You don't feel accepted for who you are, only for how you
perform. You grow up with a feeling of resentment because
you were never good enough to win your father's full approval.
This sense of doubt can linger for years without resolution
because you don't want to face rejection from your father at
any age.

Some men feel that their mother's love also was contingent
upon their successful performance. Our society promotes the
so-called "masculine" values of rational thinking, specialization
and the pursuit of perfection. Men are encouraged to seek perfection by isolating and exaggerating some aspects of their

personality and excluding others. A more intuitive approach to living values the intelligence of our instincts and feelings as well as our thoughts. We often learn these functions through the mother, as she teaches us how to care for ourselves. When we honor our instincts and feelings, we know when we are tired, comfortable, truly receiving love, and so forth. Due to their own upbringing, some mothers did not bond with people who valued their feeling, intuitive function. These mothers will be unable to support that function in their sons and daughters. If your parents did not learn to balance their energies, you will probably have to develop this sense in yourself as part of learning to nurture yourself.

You may compensate for a lack of love in different ways. Some people mistrust love and become excessively aloof, while others strive to be overachievers to gain acceptance. You may try to please others all the time as a form of compensation. All of these are misconceptions about the true nature of love.

You need to acknowledge your need for love before you can receive it. First, you must be loving to yourself. Accept yourself unconditionally for who you are. Then learn to share love. And finally, forgive your parents, especially your father, for not showing you the love he felt. One way to do this is by writing a letter to your father. The letter will serve its purpose whether or not he accepts it, because you are the one who needs the healing. By forgiving your father, you free yourself.

What are you willing to sacrifice to be who you really are?

A real man must stand up for his beliefs. In many cases, it will require sacrifice to do so. You must live out your beliefs, not simply exist in silence. Otherwise, by your silence, you will condone things in which you do not believe. You know that your neighbor is abusing his children, for example, but you choose to remain quiet. By not speaking out against his abuse, you have compromised your basic principles. Men don't like to live at less than their potential. There's no pride in that, no self-respect or self-esteem.

You don't have to accept that your conditioning was right or normal. You don't have to do things just to appease other people. You need to stand up for your ideals, even in the face of adversity. Otherwise, the conflict between your inner and outer selves will begin to wear you down. It can eventually lead to physical and mental illness.

Courage is all it takes to be who you are. Better to be honest about your beliefs—even if they differ from the socially accepted standards—than to suffer in silence and wreak havoc on your mind and body. If you live by your honest feelings and show true love, you will be respected and admired by other men, even if they don't express their admiration openly. You make them wonder what it is that gives you an inner peace and happiness—and what it is that they don't have themselves.

List both your good and bad qualities. Life doesn't work if you express only your good qualities and have a dark side that you do not acknowledge even to yourself. Until you face your total being, both good and bad, you can never grow. You will not be able to move forward with your life if you have any unresolved conflicts of principle because you are not a well-defined person. You will get caught up in the world of make-believe rather than in the reality of your life.

What is a balanced relationship?

A balanced relationship meets the essential needs of both people. That doesn't mean, however, that each party must give to the relationship in equal proportions. Rather, it means that you give of yourself to the best of your ability. If you give more than you reasonably can offer, or if you withhold a part of yourself, the relationship becomes imbalanced.

Take an honest look at what you need from your relationship. Do you express those needs to your partner? If you do not understand your own needs and share them with your partner, you cannot expect to have a good relationship. It's unreasonable to expect someone to recognize your needs automatically, without your saying anything. Your partner can't read your mind, after all, and you will end up feeling frustrated and angry. Honest communication is essential to a balanced relationship.

How do you know when a change comes from your real self versus your ego?

When contemplating changes in your life, remember that the ego always looks to gain advantage, while the real self simply seeks to explore and to grow. What's more, your ego generally externalizes things and blames other people for your problems. It takes the responsibility away from you. The ego would rather try to change everyone around you than to change who you are. Your real self, on the other hand, will explore your inner nature and lead to positive changes.

Do you fear death?

If you feel out of control in your life, you may develop a fear of death. This connection often occurs when people look at the past and determine that they haven't accomplished anything worthwhile. They have yet to fulfill their dreams or aspirations.

When you get up each morning, tell yourself that the day belongs to you. Say to yourself, I'm taking control. What I do today will affect my life. I'm going to use positive thoughts, deeds and actions. I'm going to actualize my higher self. I'm going to give joy, to be open and to listen carefully before I react to anything. I'm going to discard any negativity.

Throughout the day, be aware of the positive things that result from this approach. Good things will be returned to you, and this positive feedback will reaffirm your sense of control and enhance your self-esteem. Remember, too, that you need to reestablish who you really are as you take charge of each day. Don't be afraid to show your vulnerability as well as your strength. When you live fully as yourself every day, you will lose your fear of death. Death holds no power over you when you have control over your life.

Are you easily provoked to anger and other negative emotions?

Certain situations may cause you to experience negative emotions, such as anger and depression. When this occurs, you need to evaluate your response to the situation. You may be reacting according to your conditioning. Suppose, for example, that someone cuts in front of you in his car and you feel like running into him. You are the one who will suffer from the internal frustration this type of anger generates. You could just as easily recognize that the other driver's actions do not affect you.

You have the freedom to take any approach you choose to the situation. But you lose this freedom if you respond according to your conditioning. Therefore, you must overcome your conditioned responses to take a more reasoned approach. Ask yourself if there are alternative explanations for another's behavior. Imagine yourself in that person's situation. If your anger is justified, is it very important that you express it? Before you react in anger, evaluate the situation and see if the anger will make any difference or whether it is just a learned reaction.

How do you resolve pent-up emotions from childhood?

Our childhood emotions can be the underlying cause of many present-day problems. We may react adversely to people who say or do something that subconsciously reminds us of our past. For example, you may be in a relationship with a woman who reminds you of your mother. And you may end up admonishing her for your mother's shortcomings. Until you resolve your latent desire for fulfillment, you will continue to blame her for the things your mother did not provide.

Make a list of the needs, events or experiences that were overlooked or denied during your childhood. Also, list the things you missed because you had to shoulder responsibilities that your parents didn't or couldn't. These situations caused you deep-seated pain and anger that carry over to this day. You may need to evaluate the items on this list one by one to identify those things that are influencing your life, both positively and negatively. Only after you resolve the negative issues will you be able to forgive and forget so that you can live your life free of the influences of the past.

How do you handle deception and betrayal?

Everyone knows what it feels like to be deceived. And once you have been betrayed a few times, you will begin to recognize the signs of deceit early on. The person may fail to make eye contact, or he or she may assume a certain body language. Your intuition will tell you what is about to happen. This intuition can help you to avoid the same pitfalls.

Naturally, you will feel hurt when you are betrayed. However, you need to forgive the person and let the negative emotions go. Then you can get on with your life and the things that really matter.

When should you challenge authority?

You don't have to accept authority when it is self-serving and abusive. Indeed, you should challenge it. If you find yourself thinking of excuses not to act, you are allowing your insecurity and fearful, negative feelings to undermine your resolve to live by your principles.

Be wary of anyone who professes to have all the answers for you. This precaution is essential. A goal in life is to develop your own inner guide. We allow others to have an undue influence on us because we do not know ourselves or our values. When we make contact with our own higher self, we will discover that we created the illusion that other individuals and society at large have power over us.

Do you have trouble ending relationships?

If you feel trapped in a relationship that is not nurturing, and your partner appears to want to continue the relationship, then you need to examine your past. Maybe you were not allowed to say no or were not encouraged to assert yourself. Dig into your past to find the origin of these feelings. Undoubtedly, you will find that there were many such incidents in your childhood.

How do you end relationships?

When you want to end a relationship, accept responsibility for its breakdown and explain that you are not the person he or she needs you to be. Don't blame or intimidate the other person. By accepting responsibility yourself, you allow the other to save face. In some cases, this approach will leave you open to ridicule. But if the relationship ends successfully, you have accomplished your goal.

You should be in a relationship because you like being there, not because you are co-dependent. All relationships need to be based on mutual respect and positive reinforcement. That's the real reason that you should be with someone.

Do you seek help when you need it?

Men are conditioned to be loners. As a result, they have a difficult time expressing their need to be accepted and to bond with other people. To do so, they believe, would make them appear needy. Meanwhile, they grow up admiring role models who were always alone. These heroes of the past, like the cowboys, would ride off alone into the sunset. Some men will confide in one close friend, but most are reluctant to seek professional help or group support.

In the 1990s, men are finally beginning to open up and get in touch with their feelings. They are learning to express themselves with the help of professional counseling or support groups. This is a first step toward growth. See whether you get in touch with your inner feelings.

What behavior characteristics do you want to change?

Some common negative behaviors include the following (you may experience these as gut reactions or have a vague sense that they apply): You need to control all conversations; you have trouble expressing your feelings; you selectively choose what you want to hear; you hold rigidly to a point of view because you are afraid to change; you reject anything that does not fit your perspective; you maintain an image and reject whatever does not fit your self-concept; you have overcommitted yourself and feel burdened by responsibilities; you're unsure of how to do things.

Make a list of five characteristics that you would like to begin to change.

What repetitive, negative patterns do you participate in?

People who do not have control of their lives will recreate patterns of disharmony that have proven to work for them. If yelling or threatening always helps you to win an argument, then you will continue that behavior pattern. Even though the other person has become quiet out of fear, you will not attempt a more reasonable approach to handling a disagreement.

You need to find reasonable and healthy ways to communicate and live your life. That means you must respect other people. Always consider what it would be like to be on the other end of one of your conversations. Look at the long-term consequences of your actions and ask yourself, "Would this make me feel good?"

Make a list of your repetitive negative behaviors. Try to understand why other people react to you as they do. Change these behaviors into more positive ones.

Are you who you want to be?

The professional community often divides people into type A (high stress) and type B (passive) personalities, but this is an overly simplistic paradigm. Many people thrive under stress; they work day and night and socialize night and day. These people manage to commingle their personal and private lives. They create balance by doing the things they love to do.

Creative people, by their very nature, often are volatile and expressive because they allow the energy of the unconscious (the emotional, the unexpected) to disrupt the dominance of the ego. An overly strict ego or an overly structured external environment can discourage creativity. What would happen if you were to tell an artist such as Picasso or Dali that he must work from nine to five, or that he must not be so highly excitable? You would destroy the basis of their creativity. Painters and other artists need to express their internal zeal to give us their gifts of poetry, dance, music and writing.

By our willingness to adhere unquestioningly to meaningless conventions, we have dehumanized and depersonalized the society in which we live. We must not look to others to tell us who we are, what we should value, how to look, what to eat, how to feel. When Mao Tse-tung's cultural revolution sought to set universal norms for China's population, creative and artistic expression was suppressed. This most powerful and important source of social and personal renewal was denied, and China ended up with a sterile society.

Creative expression is the energy of life. People who have not found the courage to express themselves can easily become depressed. Long-term depression is the leading emotional disease in our society today. It is also the impetus of many physical diseases, since psychological depression decreases the body's immunity. Expressive people are seldom depressed. That is not to say that they never feel transient negative moods. People who are open to creativity and personal growth will allow all feelings into their consciousness in order to learn from them.

Begin to act on your insights. Perhaps you will find the courage to give up a nine-to-five job and start a business you really love. You may even look forward to working 12-hour days because you enjoy what you are doing. As long as you express your real feelings and maintain balance in your life, you will thrive.

When you change, you challenge the reality of people around

you. People close to you may feel unsettled by your new energy level, or they may feel that your relationship with them is threatened by your freedom and self-expression. They may envy your ability to tap your creativity. But you should not let the negative reactions of others hinder your growth. Your courage may ultimately prompt those around you to make positive changes as well.

Men are beginning to realize that they have been complacent for too long. They would go to the ballpark and scream and yell, but, for fear of losing their jobs, they suffered in silence if their work conditions were unhealthy. They would go to church and sit by passively, never questioning or challenging anything as they muttered an occasional "amen" and "pass the till."

Finally, men are accepting responsibility for what they must say and share with others in order to express their creativity and add meaning to their lives. As this trend continues, there will be less anxiety, less abuse, less alcoholism and drug addiction, and more family harmony.

Make a list of the times you suppressed your creativity or were unresponsive to situations that really required your attention. Then make a list of the times you expressed your real feelings in a meaningful and caring way for your own benefit or that of your fellow man.

Do you struggle for power?

Are you out there struggling to accumulate power, or do you recognize the natural power that each of us possesses? You need power so that you can live your life, but if you assume you don't have it you will let someone else have power over you.

To use your inherent power, all you really need to do is make a decision about what you are willing to do for yourself and the ideals in which you believe. People often try to make you feel that you are not empowered in life. If you believe that, you won't make decisions on your own. You will be conditioned by society. You'll eat the four basic food groups, for example, which has been a major contributor to disease for the past 50 years. Even as you're eating yourself to death, you will believe that you're doing the right thing by following these food guidelines. A more rational—and empowered—approach is to make your own decisions about the right and wrong foods to eat.

You need to follow your intuition. When you feel that something is right but the structured power around you says it's not, follow your instincts and go by your own experience. It's only when you stand up for yourself that you can use your power in a constructive way. Otherwise, someone else will use power against you.

Are you egotistical?

Do you believe it's important to satisfy your ego? Many people seem to think so. Consider all the executives who do not hobnob with the general society. Instead, they display the trappings of success by frequenting exclusive clubs, elite restaurants and exotic resorts. They drive expensive cars and own extravagant homes with many more rooms than they need. They pay high prices for these homes so that they can live in exclusive neighborhoods and display their social status. In short, they do anything to get the merit badges of life.

Most men seem to have a great need to be acknowledged. They're always looking for recognition, either through their business life, where they become high-powered executives, or through their recreational activities, where they become the head of the bowling league or the softball team. They want to have something that you don't have.

Occasionally you will find a man who simply hangs out with life and enjoys it to its fullest, with no need to impress anybody. This takes a mature, balanced, whole person. In the past, our nation had many such men. But with the advent of the Doctor Spock baby-boomers came the philosophy that everybody had to be a winner. Men adopted compulsive behavior and put the pedal to the metal to get as far ahead as they could, as fast as they could.

The baby-boomer generation raised and spent three trillion dollars with very little to show for it except a lot of debt, pain and destroyed lives. The greatest amount of cocaine addiction in history occurred within this upwardly mobile group, which used the drug for a supposed energy boost. The baby-boomer's destructive dependence on drugs and alcohol was no accident; it was concurrent with their need to achieve.

In today's society, people are under a tremendous amount of stress. We have become a nation of emotionally stunted people because we have believed in things that we do not need. We overconsume to prove to others that we have significance, all based on the fact that we're really very insecure. A man who is comfortable being a man doesn't have to overextend himself. He doesn't have to prove anything. People intent on proving that they're acceptable often try so hard that, ultimately, they never achieve that goal and never feel content with life.

Do you have the time and patience to be who you really are?

American men have become very impatient. They want material possessions now—and more of them than they can possibly use. They're willing to get themselves into debt to show that they deserve these things. Once they assume this debt, however, they don't handle the pressure well and start breaking down. They resent having things they don't really need, and they generally punish themselves and others for this state of affairs.

Americans have become gluttonous. They're out of shape, lazy, unfocused, undisciplined and unhappy. This is the most addicted society in history—one that has spawned tremendous anger. Hostility is manifest all around you through exhibitions of violence, particularly in sports such as football, the roller derby, gladiators and wrestling.

This cycle of gluttony and anger doesn't occur as much in cultures where men are happy about being men. They're content with their lives. We can take a lesson in patience from other cultures. Maybe what many American men need to do is take a trip to Europe. If you were travel to Milan, Florence or Venice, you would see that men there are physically fit. These men have a passion for life; they express themselves openly and with vitality. They are never in a hurry. At noon, they close down their businesses to join their family for a meal, a short siesta and a relaxing conversation, and afterwards they return to their work rejuvenated. They usually work until about seven at night, have a light dinner, and then enjoy their family and social life for the rest of the evening. You won't find them vegetating in front of the television set because these people have a zest for life. They're eternally romantic and express passion in everything they say and do.

Further into the countryside, you will find villagers in their 80s and 90s who still tend their flocks, their gardens or their grandchildren every day. They live in small communities of four to ten homes that are separated by farmland from the next hamlet. Thousands of these small communities dot the countryside. This is where the population at large lives.

These people have a reason for living. When you ask them what that reason is, they say that they really enjoy life. They certainly don't have fancy cars and all the latest gadgets. They're not rich and they don't have money in the bank, but none of this worries them because they know they have a reason for living when they rise each day. They've learned to master what they do. Craftsmanship takes time, patience, understanding and apprenticeship. You see men in the countryside weeding their gardens with the precision of a Zen gardener. They don't try to rush nature. They live within a natural time frame. You can't pull on a rose to make it grow at an unnatural pace. Everything will happen when it needs to happen.

List all of the things you do on a daily basis. Are you an expert in any of them? Maybe you should identify the ones that are important to you, and then devote more time and attention to perfecting them. Eliminate some of the others that have little meaning in your life.

Are you cluttering up your life with material things?

Look at all the material possessions in your life. Identify those you really don't want, need and use, and then get rid of them. Give things away. Let other people enjoy what you've long lost the ability to appreciate.

Once you give something away, don't bring in a substitute right away to take its place. Rather, learn to scale down. It's better to have less debt and more freedom than to be enslaved to new things you do not need. Use this new-found freedom to take care of your real needs, to create real priorities for yourself and to make better use of your precious time.

When you start letting go of the things that no longer serve you, you begin to lighten your load in life. There's an old saying that those who want to travel far in life must travel light. When compiling your list of things that you no longer use or need, include the clothes you haven't worn in years, the TV set you haven't turned on for months, and the old tires in the garage that do not fit your car. Think of people who could make use of these items.

Are you living in the present?

It's fine to have long-term objectives, but if all your goals are in the distant future, you may never get around to enjoying them. Why put your life on hold? Instead, begin to view each day as special—one that you won't have next week or next year. Life is short and you never know when it will end. That doesn't mean you should live irresponsibly, but it does mean that you must recognize that today counts.

Make a commitment to put your energies into today. By living your life one day at a time, you reaffirm your choices and live life to the fullest. No matter what comes, you will make each day a constructive one in your life. Every morning when you get up, look at life and see what positive thoughts and actions you can take to confirm your legacy. Can I do something for others? Can I be patient? Can I be compassionate? Can I take care of my own mind and body? Can I allow myself to grow? Can I be intimate and open with others? Can I live with what's in my heart? You can do all of these things.

Once you set these ideas in motion, they will become a pattern of behavior that works for you. You will start to feel more relaxed, light, confident, honest and flexible. You will have a much greater range of intellectual and emotional happiness. Make a list of the things that matter in your life. Are you doing these things now and living a positive, dynamic life, or are you always planning for some time that may never come in the far-distant future?

Intrinsic love is the energy that allows life to thrive. Ultimately, you must choose what type of a life you want and how you want to live it. It's a choice you make by deciding to be consistent and positive. All the right situations in the world will not grow if they are not nurtured by love.

How do you view life?

Some people believe they are a victim of circumstances. Good and bad things just happen to them, no matter what they do. Other people believe that their active participation in life helps to shape their circumstances. With the second philosophy, you take an entirely different approach to living. You are more likely to wake up each day and affirm your needs, knowing that your conscious effort makes a real difference in each day's events.

You might face the mirror each morning and say, "Thank you, God, for this day. I'm glad to be alive because this moment is the only one that I can really change." This attitude allows you to focus on an immediate concern, such as the need to change the way you eat, the way you live, the people you live with, the way you communicate, the way you spend time and so forth.

This approach to life will give you a different mindset. It is an important prerequisite for changing your life because it emphasizes the things that are important to you. There will always be some things that you cannot control, of course. But you will feel greater harmony in any situation if you believe that your life is in control. Suppose that you get stuck in a traffic jam. If you change your perception of the experience, you will feel less impatient and more relaxed. You have not changed the reality, but you have changed your experience of it. Make a list of the aspects of your life you need to change.

Do you exaggerate your problems?

Many people think their problems are insurmountable, when, in reality, they are just blown out of proportion. Perhaps these people have become spoiled by too many gifts and options. American welfare recipients, for example, eat more food than some of the wealthiest families in impoverished nations. Imagine that you live in a war-torn nation like Somalia, where people must fight just to survive. Owning nothing but the rags on your back, you hunt for food in the bushes at night surrounded by hyenas and lions. You don't have a home and must spend your time traveling from one battlefield to another, watching your children die from starvation. What you wouldn't do then to have your basic needs met with things you forgot were important.

If you feel resentful because you have hardships in life, you are expressing an inflated opinion of yourself. You've forgotten what real suffering is. All human beings have problems. If you find meaning in your limitations and don't make mountains out of molehills, you will gain an awareness of your strength.

Do you project your shortcomings onto others?

It is often the case that we cannot acknowledge our own shortcomings, but react strongly to the shortcomings of others. When you are feeling hypercritical, judgmental, bitter, cynical or sarcastic toward someone, stop. Take your intensely negative feelings as a signal that the very attribute that so enrages you in others may be an aspect of yourself as well.

It does not matter whether or not the other person possesses the negative attribute. What matters is that you have something to learn about yourself in this area. You probably feel as intensely intolerant toward yourself, albeit unconsciously, as you do toward the offender you have targeted. If you make an honest effort to recognize and change the conflicts in your own life—and are willing to acknowledge that you can grow beyond them—you can do so.

In addition, become conscious of any tendency you have to idealize others. In this case, you project everything positive onto others and expect them to embody the positive qualities you possess in an undeveloped state. Focus on developing your own positive qualities instead.

Do you use your time properly?

The only thing in life you can really call your own is your time. Why waste it? Use your time wisely by paying attention to your real needs, not the superficial ones that can rob you of time and energy. Take time to nurture yourself. Allow the child in you to come out and help guide you in the nurturing process.

Are you looking for love?

The idea that you must look for love is the wrong way to view this aspect of life. You are love. Love is inside of you; it's not something outside of yourself. If you open up and share your vulnerability and intimacy, you will draw people to your inner light. They will feel the love you represent. And when you meet people who are willing to do the same, you will automatically bond with these people.

Are you conditioned to react rather than to reason?

Insecure people are hypersensitive, and they retaliate easily. Others must be careful not to step on their egos or trigger their emotional minefields. These people react rather than reason, a pattern of behavior that usually starts in childhood when their parents teach them words and gestures to be used as defense mechanisms. Before long, they have been inundated with rules that cause them to react in ways that are excessive and counterproductive.

You must learn to trust your sense of reasoning. Otherwise, your exaggerated attitude toward people may generate excessive responses. Make a list of your common reactions and try to identify proper responses to be used in their place.

Do you retaliate?

Retaliation, in and of itself, is an infantile behavior. It's an inhumane way to respond to other people. When you strike back at someone, you show your need to be right at any cost. If you catch yourself thinking about retaliation, stop to consider both the reasons why and the consequences of doing so. What am I angry about? Why do I want to retaliate? What will happen if I do? How would it feel to be on the other end of what I am about to do or say? If it doesn't feel good, then you shouldn't act on this negative impulse.

Are you both competitive and cooperative?

Both of these qualities are important, and each has its place in life. In the best of circumstances, they can complement each other in a highly effective way. In long-distance races, for example, athletes often do best when they run together at first and help each other to maintain the pace. Then, at the end of the race, they run competitively.

I'll never forget a race I entered in Washington. About 15 athletes participated, all of us trying to make the national qualifying time. During the competition, a highly skilled athlete— one of the best of all times—noticed that one of the less-experienced runners was starting to pull back from the group. He gave up his lead position to help this runner.

The less-experienced racer, who was having cramps, told the other athlete that he didn't have the energy to continue. The experienced athlete helped him through that difficult stage with some guided visualization. He paced with the runner until the man was able to get back into the race. As a result, the racer who almost dropped out made the qualification time by one second. The spirit of camaraderie during a competition distinguishes a real athlete from an insecure one.

Cooperation is an important quality in all areas of life, but some men have difficulty showing it. They equate it with weakness because they fear others will take advantage of them. These men believe they must win at any cost and that any means will justify the end. They are feared by others, but at the same time they artificially isolate themselves.

Today, men are beginning to understand the need to cooperate. Being cooperative makes them more likeable as human beings. When they need help themselves, people will be more patient, tolerant and accepting of them. In the end, they get the same amount of work done and everyone involved feels they have won. They can create win-win situations.

Cooperation is especially vital to relationships. Being overly competitive is unhealthy because it promotes fear. If you always need to have the first and last word, for example, normal interactions become impossible. No matter what anyone says, you deny its value and, in effect, disempower that person. You use words defensively to control others and make them feel subservient.

When you work as a team, on the other hand, you talk openly. You realize that both people must contribute to a relationship to make it work. In any relationship, you must discuss what you feel comfortable doing, what decisions you feel comfortable making and to what degree you feel comfortable making them. This keeps the relationship balanced.

Too much competition creates a gross imbalance that affects the relationship on every level. One partner takes on too much responsibility while the other becomes overly dependent. The person who is in control makes even the most mundane decisions, like where to eat. He assumes that his decisions are always right and that his partner must enjoy the relationship because there are no complaints. But compliant people seldom complain, at least directly. They may complain to their friends over the phone or sublimate their feelings by watching soap operas, but they are afraid to speak to you face-to-face about what's bothering them. If you are overly competitive, the first step to changing your behavior is to recognize what you are doing. Can you see where you are exercising unnecessary control?

Do you go along with the group?

If you are compliant by nature, you accept the status quo without question. Your identity derives from the groups to which you give your support. Belonging to these groups makes you feel accepted. You may be the type of man who works at the post office for 40 years and never complains about the system of which he is a part. Instead of looking for things to reform, you adapt to given conditions as long as your basic needs are met. You never think of starting your own business, even if you have the financial ability to do so. You feel much more comfortable being a part of someone else's business.

People who are dynamic by nature tend to challenge the establishment and take certain risks rather than play it safe. If you are a politician, you are the maverick who takes on controversial causes, not the cautious politician looking for a guaranteed career path. If you are a doctor, you question standard medical practices and use the techniques that work for your patients even if they are not sanctioned by the medical associations.

This type of person can't comprehend working for someone else. One hour's work in a post office would be too much. You'd rather be on the street. You have a disdain for the ordinary, especially when it means sacrificing your freedom and your identity. You are a constant seeker.

These two basic types of men (or women) can be classified as supportive and dynamic. Society needs both in order to function. Without innovative men and women, we would have no one to lead the way. We would have no Frank Lloyd Wright, Robert Moses, Voltaire, Buddha nor Christ. Without supportive people, we would have no one to execute ideas. Society needs cooperation between these two groups, the dynamic and the supportive.

Do you follow your intuition?

People who do not develop their insights will pay an enormous price. Those who obey authority blindly allow totalitarian rule and fascist ideologies to exist. In Japanese culture, where the individual is subordinate to the group, people are not motivated to become autonomous because they receive all the support they need at home and at work. This support results from dedication to the work principle, which goes unquestioned and unchallenged.

American society tends to be more flexible. Here you can gain the insights you need to be both autonomous and to work with a group when necessary. But it takes some effort to do so. In the 1940s and 1950s, when people did not acknowledge their own insights, men believed that real men would only eat huge steaks and fries and other high-fat foods.

The basic-four food group diet was a major contributor to coronary heart disease and cancer, but the average man would consider it unacceptable to be a vegetarian. Men would rather weigh 250 pounds and be headed toward sickness than be a 165-pound vegetarian with normal biochemistry and health. Vegetarians were regarded as being gay or communists.

Many people are still very primitive when it comes to developing insight. But some men have indeed identified their real and honest needs. They see what they really want to be, really want to do and who they really want to do it with. They no longer feel constrained by their religious and social positions.

Do you work within your physical limitations?

You must accept your limitations before you can overcome them. When you ignore these limitations, you do yourself more harm than good. Perhaps you want to start an exercise program, but you're overweight because you have not exercised for some time. Your blood pressure is too high and your cholesterol and triglycerides are elevated. If you do not acknowledge these limitations and exercise in a reasonable way, you run the risk of dying from a heart attack or stroke.

You must honor your body's condition and realize that you cannot improve your health instantaneously. Take your time and perform the actions necessary to compensate for your limitations. You may need to have a cardiovascular stress test, an

EKG test and even a musculoskeletal examination to determine what types of exercise you can perform safely.

Do you prepare for change in your life?

Positive change requires preparation and work. The results don't simply fall into your lap. If you're not happy at work, for example, you must prepare for the job you really want. The transition may require that you train yourself, familiarize yourself with the new job and possibly advance your education so that you're the best qualified candidate for the job.

If you do not make this effort, in all likelihood, you will go nowhere. You'll complain all the time that you feel trapped in a job you do not like. You will be a perpetual victim. This is true of many men who work in the coal, steel and auto industries. A good percentage of them complain about working the same old boring job day after day at a fixed wage. But when their factory finally lets them go, they feel betrayed. They take their anger out on the union for not having negotiated a better deal.

While outside factors may contribute to your problems, you must recognize that you are ultimately responsible for your own happiness. You can't rely on your union, corporation or boss to change the things that bother you. Think of what you must do to make your life work in a meaningful way. Think of ways to overcome any limiting circumstances. If you don't, you make yourself a victim and allow others to exploit you. But once you take control of your situation and initiate the process of change, you will find that others support your efforts.

It's your choice. You can either sit around and moan at home when you get laid off or you can take positive action. Instead of drowning in self-pity and longing for your old job, use the time to rebuild your confidence. Perhaps you could get some training in another profession, one that is more to your liking and that offers a better guarantee of work.

Another option is to create a home-based business. I know one family that turned their garage into a bakery when the husband lost his job. They didn't cry in their beer and let their lives go down the drain, which would have compounded an already negative situation. Instead, they read up on baking, watched videos, took workshops, went to auctions and bankruptcy sales and put together their own small business. They began to advertise and even had their children make home deliveries.

They reasoned that they could supply higher-quality and better-priced goods than the processed junk food found in supermarkets. Starting the business gave them a sense of confidence, and over time the little bakery expanded. Today it's a thriving business.

People operate all sorts of successful home-based businesses now. Some homemakers sell crafts, others teach remedial reading to children. There are a thousand paths you can take if you choose not to be a helpless victim. Reject the status-quo mentality that says you must wait to be called back to your old job or find a similar job that offers you nothing more than a dead end. You don't have to follow standards that do not work for you.

What false assumptions do you have?

Most people live with many false assumptions. See if any of these sound familiar to you: You assume you're going to marry the right person and live happily ever after; you assume that the way you were raised is the way you should raise your children; you assume that the way you've been taught to eat in the past is the way you should eat now; you assume that your job will be there forever.

People accept such ideas as fundamental truths because of their conditioning. According to a concept known as cognitive dissonance, our early training stays with us the rest of our lives. This training, no matter how unreasonable or impractical, becomes a person's standard throughout life.

You need to examine the source of your beliefs. Ask yourself, am I really happy with the things I was taught to accept as a child? If not, what beliefs made you feel uncomfortable and unhappy? Are you passing on these very beliefs to your own children? Perhaps your mother gave you food every time you complained as a child, and to this day you eat whenever you feel upset. Becoming aware of the roots of your problems is an important first step to overcoming them. The key is to allow yourself to start over again.

What male stereotypes do you adopt?

Most American men respect an all-purpose list of "male" attributes—authority, control, power, strength, dominance and invincibility. They're terrified to show compassion, uncertainty or any sign of weakness. Thus they will quickly resort to violence to settle an issue.

Where do these images come from? Many were fabricated in Hollywood, where actors such as Marlon Brando and James Dean personified the American male hero of the 1950s—the tough, defiant loners who chose to play by their own rules.

200

There was also John Wayne, who portrayed the all-American leader protecting society's standards. His character exemplifies the typical male ego, which says that we are a first-rate power that must maintain our control at any cost.

Unfortunately, this belief has bankrupted our national economy. It has justified an overtaxation of the population, the production of arms when we have no one to fight and the production of unnecessary weapons at a time when the stockpile in our nuclear arsenal could kill every man, woman and child 47,000 times over. This system exists solely to perpetuate the male ego's concepts of strength and invincibility. To fuel the myth that such weapons are needed, people are made to feel paranoid and fearful. They believe that only their leaders can be trusted. In fact, their very lives depend upon their government's ability to guard and protect them.

But governments, much to their shame, fabricate enemies and build them into real threats for the public consumption. The United States government has made Cuba's Fidel Castro seem like a legitimate threat. The truth is that he couldn't fire off a banana peel, let alone a rocket. We could have annihilated him in about a week had we chosen to, but we needed him to perpetuate the Cold War in the Western hemisphere.

We played the same game in Nicaragua and several other Central and South American countries. But the height of this folly was in trying to make Saddam Hussein's third-class army appear to be invincible. They were such poor soldiers that they couldn't win a war with Iran in eight years despite their collection of high-tech gear. In the weeks before Desert Storm, we made them into a Goliath, as if they were a major threat to American security.

As in the past, this technique did the trick of confirming

201

that we are powerful and in control. But in the process, we devastated a country, caused the death of about 300,000 people, spent about $100 billion and caused several hundred Americans to die from our own friendly fire. After some 200,000 bombings, we left pretty much as we came and Hussein remained in power.

The male image also associates power with money; hence our fascination with men who become millionaires and billionaires, such as Donald Trump, Michael Milken and Ivan Boesky. We admire their big homes, beautiful women, fancy clothes and sports cars, and we dream of attaining these things ourselves.

We never question how these men get their money or power. We never wonder about the types of deals they make. An objective look at many of the people we admire would reveal that the takeover artists of the 1980s caused the displacement and loss of five million blue-collar jobs. Not until they were caught and convicted for overt illegal actions did we realize that they are not the great white knights we thought they were. In reality, many such men are megalomaniacs who don't care about anyone but themselves.

We have a warped male concept of success, power and control. It's based upon winning at all costs and doing everything possible to get ahead. How many hugely successful American men and their families earned their fortunes honestly or ethically? Perhaps none of them.

Do you look to others to support your ego?

Men tend to surround themselves with people who strengthen their identity and do not threaten to expose the qualities about them that they fear most. In a male-female relationship, for example, a man who is insecure about his masculinity will look for a woman who does not require him to be masculine. If you base your identity on your physical appearance, you will choose a woman who always comments on your manly appearance and flatters your ego. You won't have someone in your life who challenges you with comments such as, "Shape up, I don't like your infantile attitude. You're sexist and inconsiderate." Your partner will be an extension of your ego, whether or not your self-image is a healthy one.

A healthier relationship is one in which the partners respect each other's differences but continue to support the relationship. You help each other to recognize faults and make improvements. You may say, for instance, "Come on, now. You're exaggerating, and it's making you look foolish to other people."

Granted, it is difficult to hear the truth at times. I know someone, for example, who always embellished his conversations to make him seem a little bit better than everyone else. One time he left the room and I saw one man turn to another and say, "Isn't that unfortunate? He keeps exaggerating all the time just to get some attention."

I knew this person very well, so I asked him privately if he knew he looked foolish every time he made up a story. He became livid and did not talk to me for a year. Then one day he told me that he had finally come to terms with his compulsion to exaggerate. When I first spoke to him, he had denied his feelings because he was so fearful of them. Our relationship became stronger and healthier for this experience.

It's important to have people in your life who are honest, who will speak to you candidly without humiliating you in the process.

What motivates you to change?

Like most people, you may attempt to make changes in your life when you feel that your self-esteem is at stake. For instance, you may make a New Year's resolution to lose weight because you don't like what you see in the mirror. You feel depressed and unsettled by your appearance, so you compensate for your feelings by going on a crash diet or a faddish exercise program.

The problem is, changes based on what you do not like generally cannot be maintained. You'll adopt new behavior for a while, and then go right back to your old habits and your old appearance. A better approach is to conduct an objective evaluation of the adjustments you need to make at any given time, and then develop a realistic program for change. Consider the way you are now and the way you want to be. Then adjust your lifestyle, your perceptions and your reality accordingly to achieve those changes. With this approach to change, the effects will be longer lasting.

Do you undermine yourself?

Anything you do that has a negative effect on someone else ultimately will come back to affect you as well. You become a part of everything that you share with other people, good or bad. Think of this before you gossip about other people or attempt to undermine them. In the process, you will undermine yourself.

What's more, you will demonstrate a lack of character. I never trust anyone who gossips about others because I know they wouldn't think twice about doing the same to me. If I find out that someone has cheated or stolen from others, no matter how insignificant the incident, I keep my distance because sooner or later that person will cheat or steal from me.

Don't overlook these types of behavior in yourself and in others. They are barometers of what lies beneath the surface. You become what you express to others. If you express hate, you become that hate and disrupt your life. Conversely, when you project love, kindness, openness, sensitivity, understanding, care and compassion, you allow these qualities to come back into your life.

Do you feel threatened by love?

If you feel threatened and cut off from love, you will lead a sad and lonely existence. You won't know how to be intimate with people who enter your life. You won't know how to express your real needs and desires and to be your real self. And you will be afraid to share this undeveloped part of yourself for fear that others will perceive you as immature. It's like being afraid to open your mouth in the dentist's office when he just wants to take a look. You're terrified. You have resistance to it.

Perhaps you mistrust love because you were hurt at some point in your life. For example, you may have felt love for someone who only betrayed and abused you. At that point, you decided not to be open to love again because the consequences were so painful. Now you don't trust anyone who comes into your life. You've closed yourself off to the possibilities.

By reacting in this way, you limit your potential for future happiness. If a woman breaks your heart, and you mistrust all women from that day forward because you assume they will hurt you, you are seeing only the negative possibilities. If you drink one glass of spoiled milk, does that mean you should never drink a glass of milk again?

You may even seek out women with the same qualities as the first to confirm your worst expectations. If a woman leaves you for another man, you may decide that all women are prostitutes as a defense mechanism. You start to look for other women on 42nd Street in Times Square, where you are likely to find prostitutes. In this way you confirm your low image of all women.

A more positive response to this experience would be to look for women in healthier environments. Then you will find women who are willing to share romance, love, openness and joy. You must actively seek out the experiences you want to have in life.

Do you deny yourself the pleasure of new experiences?

Many people deny themselves new experiences because they do not want to relinquish their well-entrenched habits and old ways of thinking. Suppose that a friend invites you to the opera. You turn down the invitation at once, rationalizing that you don't need to see male dancers jumping around in tights. Besides, you think, Monday night football is on (even though you've seen it a hundred times before). In the same vein, you are likely to turn down the chance to see a folk festival, a rodeo, a poetry reading or anything out of the ordinary.

By living such a routine existence, you will deny yourself the joy and the growth that new experiences offer. You will be afraid to allow such experiences into your life because you would have to alter your perceptions. Many men fall into this pattern, allowing their lives to become stagnant after high school or college. But if you are open to new experiences, it doesn't have to be that way.

Do you have attitudes and behaviors that sabotage your health, happiness and growth?

Some of your attitudes and behaviors can prevent you from doing things that are in your own best interest. If you are somewhat lazy, for example, you might like to sit around and watch television on Saturday mornings. Then, when a friend suggests going for a jog, power walk or bicycle ride, you find it difficult to break your routine. You might get defensive and deny the benefits of exercising, and you might even overreact and make your friend feel bad for having suggested it. Since you work hard all week, you argue, you need Saturday mornings to do what you want to do. You feel upset that someone is infringing on your time and wants you to do something else.

That sort of thinking can undermine you. Why not look instead at the benefits that come from a change of pace? Ask yourself, is this something that will make me feel healthier, live longer, be happier, have more energy and be a better person? Poor attitudes and unhealthy behaviors also can sabotage your relationships at work. Let's say you feel threatened because a female co-worker is getting a promotion and you are not. To retaliate, you make sexual remarks about the woman in an attempt to dehumanize and dismiss her as nothing more than a sex object. You're trying to make her seem incompetent and incapable to others. And you're trying to show that your male insight, knowledge and intellect are superior. Of course, nothing productive will ever come from this approach.

Why do you please others?

In a relationship, doing something to please the other can be either constructive or destructive. It depends upon why you do it. If your intent is to show respect and appreciation of the other person—for example, you surprise your wife by preparing dinner for the family one night—then the action is constructive because it shows your unconditional love for her. You don't expect anything in return for your efforts.

In a co-dependent relationship, on the other hand, you will try to please your partner out of a need for acknowledgement. In that case, you are not acting from your own inner strength, direction and purpose. You are living in the shadow of someone else's life. You may fear punishment for not doing what is expected of you, or you may expect to be rewarded for your efforts. Neither reason is good.

Make a list of the things you've done to please other people and the reasons why you did them.

How do you respond when others attack your dignity?

When someone attacks your dignity—or makes you feel uncomfortable in any way—you must decide whether or not you will allow that person to control the way you feel about yourself. If you do, you are relinquishing control of your feelings to that person.

Understand that other people are entitled to like or dislike you. You have no control over that. But you can control how you regard yourself. Self-respect and acceptance of yourself come from within, not from what other people think of you.

Make a list of the feelings you have about yourself. How do you feel about the way you dress and act? Do these feelings come from you or from other people?

What are your weak points?

It seems to be human nature to focus all of our attention on our strengths. This allows us to perpetuate the false image that we are totally successful. Donald Trump, for instance, appeared to be enormously successful—and initially was—in his business dealings. But how successful was he in his marital life? He betrayed his wife by associating with another woman. That isn't success; it's failure. If he had ended his marriage and then pursued someone else, his actions would have been more acceptable.

Make a list of your weak points. You must be willing to deal with these qualities to have a whole relationship. Only by addressing them can you ultimately grow and thrive.

Dealing with Negative Emotions

8

By mastering the powerful energy of anger and putting it to work for you, you can create almost anything you want in life.

8

Do you get angry?

Everyone experiences negative emotions, such as anger, hurt and feelings of betrayal. But most people have a difficult time expressing negative feelings, particularly anger, to others. Learning to manage this emotion can be rewarding. In some cases, anger is our primary response to a negative situation; in others, it may mask other feelings that you find even more difficult to tolerate, such as shame. In the latter case, learning to express your anger constructively will help to uncover other important emotions as well. Freeing your anger will allow you to feel more energized.

You may have trouble showing anger in appropriate ways because our society does not encourage such expressions. Early on, in fact, we are conditioned to contain our anger. We learn to rationalize our silence by saying we deserve whatever is making us angry, and we believe we are powerless to change the situation. In reality, the opposite is true. Anger is a tremendous motivator when it is channelled constructively.

By joining together with other angry people, you can become

a great force for social change. When women boycotted meat in 1978 because the price was too high, the cost came down within two weeks. When people protested the use of MSG and sugar in baby food, the manufacturers took it out. When concerned citizens said that dolphins should not be caught along with yellow fin tuna, the practice was stopped.

Enormous change occurs when a few people focus their anger constructively. For this reason, those who have an investment in the status quo discourage anger. They don't want to jeopardize what they have attained. Middle and upper-middle class whites and blacks often do not speak out for fear of losing their symbols of success. But the irony is that once you are afraid to speak out, you become disempowered. When you lose your voice you become invisible. Suppressing angry feelings is ultimately destructive to your well-being. It can even make you physically sick. One way or another, you must learn to validate your anger and express it properly.

Think of something that angers you. Write it down. Does this anger motivate you to change the situation in a constructive way? If you are suppressing your anger, think of an appropriate way to express it instead. What first step can you take?

Why do you get angry?

You may experience anger for a variety of reasons. Some of these include:

- Feeling powerless
- Being victimized
- Failing to communicate
- Getting defensive

- Feeling betrayed
- Feeling hurt
- Feeling attachment and loss
- Feeling guilty
- Having unresolved conflicts
- Feeling insecure
- Having your beliefs violated

Feeling powerless

In this case, you feel angry when you cannot control your circumstances. An example: You are being audited by the IRS. A stranger is sitting across from you who in all likelihood will access a penalty against you for something you have not done. You feel frustrated, fearful, powerless and, ultimately, angry in the face of this bureaucracy.

Write about a situation in which you feel powerless. It could be something that happened to you as a child or something occurring in the present. Get in touch with your anger. Express these feelings on paper.

Being victimized

Victimization causes a deep and persistent anger. Children who are victims develop especially strong feelings of anger that may surface in unhealthy ways later in life. It may take a lot of work to resolve such feelings. People who were sexually abused as children, for example, may have difficulty having healthy sexual relationships as adults. Each sexual encounter reminds them of their victimization, sometimes subconsciously. They need to do much work alone or in groups to let go of their past. Otherwise their anger will continue to manifest in unhealthy ways.

Think of a situation in which you felt victimized. It can be a major life trauma or something small. Get in touch with the anger this event stirs in you. How did you react to the event? How did you use your anger? Did you resolve the situation constructively? If not, what steps can you take to do so now?

Failing to communicate

When someone does not communicate with you, or vice versa, the indifference will create anger. Conversely, you show others that you care by communicating openly. This approach to a relationship is healing. Recently a newspaper article told of a domestic fight between the head of a ballet company and his wife. The husband was arrested for becoming violent with his wife when she refused to talk about their failing relationship. How much violence in the world would be avoided if we communicated openly and honestly?

Think of a person in your life with whom you have trouble communicating. How does that obstacle anger you? Write down what you would like to say to that person.

Getting defensive

People in powerful positions who must protect their image will become defensive and angry if challenged. I see this all the time with doctors. Recently, for example, I stated on a radio show in New York City that the HIV virus alone could not cause AIDS, since many people with the disease do not have HIV. A doctor on the show insisted this was impossible, but a short time later my findings were confirmed. It was made publicly known that HIV was not a necessary component of AIDS. But the doctor never admitted he was wrong because his ego was hurt. An empowered person would have been more open.

Write about a situation that made you angry. Was your ego involved, or were you expressing your true beliefs and facing someone else's ego? In what way did either of you become defensive? Try to make an honest assessment of the situation.

Feeling betrayed

No one likes to be betrayed, especially by someone they trust. You feel hurt and angry by the experience and lose all faith in that person. You wonder when they will lie to you next. It's important at such times to express your anger to the person. Don't hide your feelings, be honest.

Feeling hurt

I was on a television show once when a man launched a vicious verbal assault against me. I had never been attacked in that way before and I didn't know how to react. Afterward, he laughed to someone that he had made mincemeat out of me on the air. I walked up to him and said, "You denigrated me because I wasn't willing to engage in a verbal attack. I wanted to deal with issues. Why did you insult me in that way?" He answered, "That's how you win."

I came away feeling very hurt. I felt as if my intellectual and spiritual sanctity had been violated, and I felt a lot of anger. But I soon realized an important lesson. I didn't have to be like that person. In fact, in his folly he showed me the tools I needed to gain strength. I learned that strength comes from humility, not from arrogance. I learned that people who attack others just to look strong are really very weak.

Recall a time when someone hurt you. Did you turn the

anger in on yourself or did you express your feelings openly? Were you able to separate yourself from the person attacking you and not absorb it? How have you become wiser from the experience?

Feeling attachment and loss

The more attachment you feel toward a person or thing, the more its loss will provoke anger. Think of the times in your life when you experienced the loss of a job, a friend or a loved one. If the loss angered you, then you were measuring your success by the things you had accumulated. You felt these people and things made your life more secure.

You need to examine all the losses in your life. Did you feel angered by loss or were you able to let go and move on? In times of loss, it may help you to make this affirmation, "When one door closes, a bigger and better one opens."

Feeling guilt

In today's society, we feel a lot of pressure to conform to narrow, specialized roles. Societal attitudes often are reinforced within the family unit, and people are encouraged from all sides to feel guilty about being different or expressing what is unique to them. Guilt makes us feel controlled or manipulated; hence, it is a primary source of anger. It makes you afraid to take risks, to challenge yourself and to grow. It keeps you in line with thoughts such as, "Good boys don't do this, and good girls don't do that." It negates anything on the other side of the accepted paradigm, including joy, happiness and new horizons. How has guilt kept you under control? Can you get in touch with the anger fueling that guilt?

Having unresolved conflicts

When someone says or does something that you believe is wrong, you may internalize the conflict and start an argument in your head. The many things you should and should not have said will run through your mind, and you may berate yourself for not having had the courage to stand up to the other person. You're angry with that person but you're equally angry with yourself. You feel like a coward.

The problem with this response to conflicts, however, is that you are listening to the wrong voice. The negative voice inside you has been allowed to supersede its positive counterpart. That negative voice has enormous power to mute the positive voice and prevent it from having an equal say.

In this way, you can carry multiple unresolved conflicts with you through life. And when you finally do express yourself from this passive position, the response is generally out of context. You may express such rage that you end up hurting yourself and others. Needless to say, you can never solve your problems constructively in this manner.

Think of an unresolved conflict in your life. Meditate on the situation. What does your higher self say to you about it? If any negative voices or feelings appear, ignore them. Can you accept that you did the best you could at the time?

Feeling insecure

Insecurity breeds anger. By definition, co-dependent people are insecure and, therefore, angry. But they suppress their anger to maintain a stable relationship. Their anger then manifests in unhealthy ways. What are you insecure about? What makes you angry? How do you manifest your anger? What steps can you take toward feeling more secure?

Having your beliefs violated

Your beliefs provide you with a sense of security. Thus, you feel threatened the moment someone challenges them, no matter how gently. You become defensive and angry. The more you have invested in your ego, the greater your need to be right. Being right becomes more important than doing right. Much conflict in the world today stems from this source.

What types of challenges to your belief systems upset you? Why do they make you feel uncomfortable? Picture yourself in your challenger's shoes. Can you see his perspective on the issue? Why or why not?

How does your anger manifest?

When you are angry inside, the emotion may express itself in many ways, some more healthy than others. The more common manifestations of anger include:

- Rage and aggression
- Repression, suppression and sublimation
- Disease
- Passive-agressive behavior

Rage and aggression

Rage is a destructive expression of anger. When you express rage, you can become very imbalanced. Rage can escalate into violence, as often happens with street gangs.

219

Repression, suppression and sublimation

Rather than express rage outwardly, most people turn the feeling inward. This type of suppression can be devastating because it allows the rage to eat away at you. It can cause you to become sick and dysfunctional.

People usually cope with anger in dysfunctional ways. You may try to feel something other than anger by throwing yourself into unproductive activities, such as compulsive sex, eating, drinking or drug addiction. Perhaps you become a workaholic, complying with an inner voice that says you can make the anger go away by doing your work perfectly. At the same time, though, you will feel even more angry at the inner tyrant who will not allow you to rest. You may sublimate your anger by committing your life to a cause that is likely to be related in some way to the primary source of your anger. Or you may spend too much time watching television, listening to the radio or talking to people. You keep busy so you don't have to feel your anger.

Many people displace feelings of rage by watching violent contact sports, such as boxing, football and hockey, or by watching violent movies. By supporting the aggressive actions of others, you sublimate your own rage. Why do you think most people supported the Gulf War? Do you think they really cared about Saddam Hussein or the political issues involved?

Do you identify with any of these forms of expressing, repressing, suppressing or sublimating rage? If so, write down some ideas for more constructive ways of dealing with your anger. Recognize that these dysfunctional behaviors will disempower you and prevent you from getting to the root of the problem. Instead, you must get in touch with who and what makes you angry. Write down what you are truly angry about. You can even write a letter to your parents or another important person in your life expressing this anger. Delivering the letter is not important; what counts is to actively recognize your anger.

Disease

Due to the connection between mind and body, disease and anger go hand in hand. Truly happy people have far fewer diseases than unhappy people. Therefore, you need to think about the ways in which your anger affects you physically. Try to resolve the problems and issues that create mental pressure before they can affect your health.

Passive-aggressive behavior

Many people withdraw from their anger and deny its existence. This often happens as you age, especially if you have not had a fulfilling life. But the denial of anger can lead to passive-aggressive behavior. You smile on the outside but feel angry on the inside. Your negativity expresses itself in behaviors for which you cannot be clearly blamed but that cause distress for others. For example, do you overcommit yourself and then drag your feet about doing what you said you would do? Do you make nasty comments and then tell the other person that you were only joking?

Think of ways that you deny your anger and withdraw into yourself. Can you get in touch with what you are denying? Can you identify any passive-aggressive behaviors you exhibit? What first steps can you take to changing a negative life situation into a more positive one?

How have you dealt with anger in different stages of your life?

As a child, teenager, young adult, adult and mature adult, how have you processed anger? Note the different behavioral patterns in which you have engaged. For each stage of life, determine when your anger caused you to react to situations and when it motivated you to take action and make positive changes.

What does and does not work in your life?

Make a list of the things that work in your life. This exercise will help you to see that control empowers you. It makes you feel positive about yourself and allows you to deal with issues in a constructive way. Then make a list of the areas of your life that do not work. You should be able to respect what works and focus your attention on what does not.

What fears do you have?

Some of your fears are realistic, others are not. Unrealistic fears are conditioned, such as the fear of trying something new. A woman with grown children who stops herself from going back to school to further her education has a fear of trying something new and different. She is allowing her growth to be limited by unrealistic fear.

Don't give all of your fears legitimacy. Learn to distinguish between fears that are reasonable and those that are not. Once you expose your fears for what they are, you will be taking a first step toward eliminating them.

Why do you suppress anger?

The thought of rejection may cause us to suppress our anger because we want to be liked and accepted by others. We may silence our anger because we do not want to be punished for expressing our true feelings. When I oppose policies of the Food & Drug Administration, for example, I run the risk of making them act more aggressively and maliciously toward me. Most people do not want to deal with such hostility. You may feel exactly as I do on certain issues, but you suppress your anger because you fear the consequences.

Perhaps you are afraid that anger will cause you to lose control and hurt someone. But this will only happen if you are full of rage and destructive anger. When your anger is justified and focused, it can only be healing to express it. Our society uses control to keep you from speaking out in your best interests. Losing control is healthy if it turns a negative situation into a positive one. Consider the environmental movement of recent years. Anger directed in a beneficial way has led to many constructive changes in our environment.

Notice the ways in which you suppress anger. What types of situations cause you to suppress your feelings? What are your reasons for keeping it in? Write down actions you can take to express that anger in a constructive way.

Have you found healthy ways to express hurt and anger?

From this point on, resolve to deal with your anger in healthy ways that will lead to positive changes. By mastering the powerful energy of anger and putting it to work for you, you can create almost anything you want in life. Here's how you can start this process of self-expression:

- Be honest with yourself
- Seek support
- Focus on the problem
- Direct your anger
- Think first
- Be active, not passive
- Act, don't react
- Don't hurt anyone
- Let go of pain and fear
- Stop compulsive behavior
- Give up perfectionism
- Learn new responses
- Organize your life
- Act in your best interests
- Make your word your bond
- Set attainable goals
- Take charge of your life

Be honest with yourself

Have an honest dialogue with yourself each morning about what is bothering you. Give yourself the time to reflect on these issues in a place where you will not be distracted.

Seek support

Share your feelings with someone who will understand your needs and your reason for being angry without criticizing or judging you.

Focus on the problem

Evaluate one problem at a time. Keep your energy focused on finding and promoting solutions until the problem is resolved.

Direct your anger

Your ability to channel anger can make all the difference in whether your feelings are positive or negative. Properly directed, anger can be a driving force in your life. But if channelled incorrectly, it can become mentally and physically destructive.

There are many avenues for expressing anger constructively. An artist, for example, can use his or her work to express anger and frustration toward society. Think of what a protest would be like without artists' posters, folk singers' songs and poets' verses. Its perspective would be limited without these constructive expressions of anger.

Think first

The old adage that tells us to count to ten when we feel angry has a great deal of merit. Reflection allows you to think before you react. You can consider what you want to say, why you want to say it and what will happen when you do. You can think through your options and react in a rational way. In the process, you free yourself from conditioning responses and focus on those that will improve the situation.

Much of your pain emanates from your conditioning. Think about the origins of this conditioning. How can you change your perceptions? If certain words or gestures upset you more than they do other people, this is due to your conditioning.

The key to resolving such conflicts is introspection. It allows you to determine the sources of these conflicts and the purpose they actually serve. It gives you an opportunity to become aware of old patterns of behavior that are destructive to you and to replace them with more positive ones. Through introspection we become more acutely aware of the inner workings of our minds and emotions.

Be active, not passive

If you are passive in a situation that calls for action, your submissiveness will allow other people to take advantage of you. And this experience, in turn, will breed even more anger. Take action to resolve such situations. Seek support if necessary.

Act, don't react

Every time something angers you, ask yourself whether you will act or react to it. Being active allows you to maintain a sense of focus; being reactive does not.

Don't hurt anyone

Uncontrolled anger can lead to violence on many levels. Domestic violence results from unmitigated anger, while war results from the egotism of leaders. Conflicts should be resolved before anyone suffers. As the saying goes, "First, do no harm." When something angers you, try to remove yourself from the situation. Think of yourself as a referee in the altercation. Call time out. What would you ask these people to do before they engage in conflict? By taking a few seconds to remove yourself from direct conflict, you will be able to evaluate the situation more fairly.

Let go of pain and fear

When your pain and fear no longer serve you, learn to let go of them. By doing so, you will be free to express yourself constructively. Remember that you cannot feel freedom until the pain is removed; these opposing feelings cannot exist at the same time.

Look at the causes of your pain and fear. Examine these feelings and say, "You've been with me for a long time but I no longer need you. I'm going to try something else." Let it go, knowing that something better will take its place. Continue to reaffirm this goal and you will find a way to accomplish it.

Stop compulsive behavior

You know when you are about to act compulsively. It doesn't just happen on its own. You don't open the refrigerator and eat a three-pound cake without knowing it, for example. You know exactly what you plan to do, and then you do it. Therefore, you should be able to stop compulsive impulses the moment they start. Have a constructive dialogue with yourself. Say, "Hold on. This is the wrong voice. There is no way I'm going to listen to you. You have no power or control over me. I'm in control of my life now. Good-bye." When you refrain from compulsive actions, they will eventually begin to go away. And you will create new, positive habits to replace these compulsions.

Give up perfectionism

You may pursue perfection to justify living in an imperfect world. But this urge will make you angry with yourself and the rest of the world. Stop looking for perfection and look instead at the realities of life. You must be honest about who you are because that's your starting point. Evolve from there and don't be impatient. You can't force a rose to grow on schedule. It grows when it is ready to do so, according to the laws of nature.

Learn new responses

If you always react according to the same old formulas, learn to respond to life in new ways. You can write your own script in life and make active choices. How will this script be different from the one you were given? This is your chance to eliminate the things that do not work for you, such as the dictates of your upbringing, your education and the way you relate to others. Of course, you can't alter events that have already occurred. But you can redirect your life from this point on.

Organize your life

Get rid of the junk that clutters up your life. It feels good to eliminate things you don't need. Pack it away, give it away, throw it away—whatever it takes to start fresh. Clean up your desk, your closet, your car and your body. The physical world reflects the mind. To respect your environment is to respect yourself. By clearing your surroundings and getting organized, you will rid yourself of the clutter and some built-up anger as well.

We're foolish not to organize our lives. We need certain systems to make things work. If a person's desk is cluttered, it may indicate that he or she does not feel comfortable with order. Order, after all, means you're getting something done. You have a beginning, middle and end. You plan to follow through on what you start, not leave calls unanswered and projects sidetracked. You're going to start something, create a blueprint for finishing it, stay focused and get it done.

Some people have trouble getting started because they know from experience that an inner voice will criticize their every imperfect effort. You must change this scenario. Get started, no matter what. Ignore your negative voice. If necessary, it can speak to you later. You're not going to be compulsive or obsessive. You're not going to push yourself beyond normal limits and judge yourself and others harshly by how something gets done. What makes a difference is that it gets done. But it doesn't happen unless we are organized.

Ask yourself where you are lacking in organization. Is it discipline? Do you feel uncomfortable when you know that you will not follow through on a specific task? A lot of writers never finish books or articles. They sit down, they get fidgety, they go to the refrigerator. They look for the phone to ring or they turn on the television to distract themselves. Many people spend too much time distracting themselves. Those who accomplish things are the ones who get organized and then focus in until the task gets done.

Act in your best interests

Make a list of the things you do that do not serve your interests. Why do you take these actions, and who benefits from them? Don't be afraid to break the old patterns you created when you were acting out of guilt or fear. Concentrate on doing things that will benefit you.

Make your word your bond

People become disenchanted when they cannot trust what you say. Then you have nothing on which to establish or maintain relationships. Frightened or insecure people are particularly prone to lying about who they are. They feel their true selves are not acceptable, so they lie about what they feel and do. A related maneuver, typical of teenagers, is to lie to feel independent and in control. While knowing that she must become autonomous, the child may fear that autonomy will alienate her parents. She does what she wants, but hides any behavior of which her parents may disapprove.

This pattern can repeat itself in adulthood. People may lie because they fear that being an individual will lead to negative feelings in a relationship. They may lie to feel the power of being the only one to know the whole story. Or they may feel so disempowered in life that they lie whenever the opportunity presents itself. They believe they have no resources within themselves to bring good things into their lives. There are no good reasons for lying. All spiritual traditions warn against it because lying impedes the development of the self and true relationships with others.

Unfortunately, lying has become the norm in today's society. Many people use words as a means to an end, with little regard for the commitment that goes with them. A prime example of this schism is a political campaign and its ultimate results. You must stand by your word, even if it is based on a bad decision. It forms the basis of your integrity and serves as a foundation on which to build your self-worth and self-esteem.

Your word reflects your values to others; it shows that you are trustworthy. Suppose that you misprice something you plan to sell based upon an incomplete analysis of the relevant factors. Someone takes you up on the offer and you accept. It is your responsibility to stand by that price, even if it costs you time or money to do so. As you go through life, you must leave a legacy of being true to your word. People will respect you for it. While others cannot expect miracles from you, they can surely ask that you keep your word.

Set attainable goals

Don't overwhelm yourself by attempting to change too much at once. You will only revert to your old habits. Instead, take one bad habit at a time and replace it with a good one. If you maintain a schedule, you have a much better chance of turning your life around. You may decide to eliminate one bad habit a week. If you are trying to improve your diet, you could eliminate sugar the first week, meat the second, caffeine the third, and so forth. Or you might work at a slower pace, eliminating one item every two or three weeks. The point is to make your goals attainable and the results evident.

Take charge of your life

There comes a time when you must redirect your spirit and intellect to develop the persona you will project the rest of your life. That means you will have to be responsible for all of your actions all of the time. You will have to stop living like a wart-hog, take chances and choose the options that move your life in a more powerful and positive direction. Now is the time to get going and do it.

Beating Self-Defeating Habits

The person who can let go of the past and move forward is the one who will find life most rewarding and exciting.

9

Are you carrying other people's burdens?

Are you always trying to second-guess someone who has not given you clear instructions? Are you frustrated because you can never please the other person? Do you feel you are inadequate at work because no matter how hard you try you're chastised for doing something that's not quite right? Is your motivation undermined because your successes are never acknowledged? Do you have to beg for acceptance on a daily basis?

If you grew up under such conditions—or now work within them—you no doubt feel insecure. But you are far from alone. American businesspeople tend to be severely critical of those they supervise. Your work isn't good enough, right enough or consistent enough to please them. It's one thing to meet attainable goals; another thing to strive to attain artificial values set by people who feel inadequate themselves and are trying to put their shortcomings off on others.

Always be on the lookout for people who continually berate you and never show any appreciation of your accomplishments.

Beware the person who wants you to be more than you can reasonably be.

Do you have problems helping someone?

Have you ever tried to teach others a simple task and found that they never quite get it, even after repetitive trials? The problem does not stem from their intellect, but rather from their belief system. They simply do not accept what you are saying. In such cases, we must have honest two-way communication and allow others to be who they are. Otherwise we may develop a co-dependent relationship. They will not change their beliefs for the long term, but merely adapt to us.

When you interact with someone like this, always watch to see how they respond. No matter what they say, you have to watch what they do. If they don't respond to your direction, it's best not to chastise them. Recognize that their beliefs may be hard to identify, confront and relinquish. They may truly want to learn from you, but at the same time they are frightened by a new belief system. If a person says he wants to be healthy but continues to eat a terrible diet, he probably believes that what he eats cannot really hurt him. You can see that his words and actions do not coincide, but the contradiction is not evident from his point of view.

To bring about change, you must develop a two-way dialogue. It never helps to force your will on others. It may take time and effort on your part, but you must help them to modify their belief system and integrate it with your own. If this happens, the changes that occur will be valid within their belief systems. If this does not occur, accept that their beliefs, for whatever reason, differ from your own. Respect this difference and allow them to maintain their autonomy. There is never only one right way to do anything. One religion or system of wellness will not suit everyone, and each human being is entitled to his beliefs without being ridiculed.

List any problems that you have had in this area and write down your observations. See if a lack of two-way communication has contributed to the problem. Can you see a way that the other's beliefs can be integrated with your own?

Do you have disparities in your own beliefs?

Do you think or say one thing and do another? If so, you need to watch yourself to determine where you are imbalanced. Your belief systems derive from your intellect, intuition and conditioning. If your feelings and intelligence tell you that a situation is wrong for you, but you do nothing physically to change it, then you have an imbalance.

The more extreme the imbalance, the worse its manifestation will be. If you stay in a bad relationship or work situation, you will feel uncomfortable even though you have rationalized that it is the right thing to do. You may even become physically sick if the discomfort continues for a long period of time. Some people, however, are totally unaware that their lives must be in balance. They feel safer adapting to a bad situation than identifying their real needs. They never ask themselves if their actions and choices fit with their personal ideologies.

Consider the creative person who needs time and space to pursue his craft. Since it's tough to pay the bills in our society on pure art, the artist may have to compromise his principles by taking a job on Madison Avenue. There, he must produce artificial, self-deprecating artwork to sell harmful products, such as cigarettes, and work under extremely stressful conditions. It's no wonder that Madison Avenue has such a high rate of turnover.

This person may rationalize that the job is not forever. But every day that he must compromise his integrity, he becomes more and more angry. Eventually, he will begin to attack his personal values with the artificial values he has been made to accept. He will start to make excuses for himself, such as, "I don't have enough money to support myself on my own" or "I'm not a good enough artist yet, so I'll do this just for a little while." Little by little, he gives up a part of his life.

To have true health, you must be balanced on all levels. You must be in tune with your real needs and react to them in a positive way. And you must look for creative solutions to your needs instead of giving in to your fears. Make a list of your genuine beliefs and refocus your agenda on them.

Do you examine the systems in which you believe?

You may be placing the blame for problems on a variety of potential culprits when the fault really lies with the system you have accepted. For example, many people in the 1980s wanted to build up home equity, generally because they were insecure. When real estate prices fell in the early 1990s, they were wiped out financially because they had bought into a system of beliefs that created artificially high prices.

The real value of property was no longer critical; it only mattered what people thought it was worth. The same belief prevailed before the Great Depression, which was caused not by economic collapse but a lack of confidence. The economy of 1929 and 1930 was booming, but everybody wanted to get rich without having to work for it. They bought stock with only ten percent down and expected to make millions of dollars.

Speculators would buy up companies with small profit margins and boost their value 40 or 50 times. When the average man saw this taking place, he bought in while the values were going up. Soon enough, however, the speculators would pull out. The little man was left to think the prices were still on the rise when in fact they were heading south. Eventually, values dropped to their true level and the game collapsed. This started a widespread panic over all the artificially inflated values.

The same thing happens again and again. For instance, ten years ago in New Jersey an acre of land worth $2,000 suddenly was valued at $50,000 or $60,000. People snatched it up, convinced that its value would double each year. They financed most of it and then waited for a million-dollar payoff. But history repeated itself and the property finally dropped to its real value.

Any belief system with artificial values will eventually have its day of reckoning. Make a list of your values. In your belief system, what has real value and what has inflated value? Challenge the ones that have inflated value.

Do you feel threatened by change?

Perhaps, like most people, you find ways to justify your resistance to change. You may deny that you need to change at all when you feel threatened. But think about what precipitates the feeling of threat. Many people don't like to acknowledge their mistakes and therefore have a fear of failure. If they were to try something new and fail, they would focus on the failure rather than give themselves credit for having tried.

Take the person who wants to stop smoking but avoids this positive but difficult task because she believes she will only start smoking again. She justifies her fear of failure by believing she will not get cancer. In fact, she may believe that cigarettes do not cause cancer. Only after she is diagnosed with the disease will she give up the habit. Unfortunately, people in our society do not learn by prevention. Most wait until the worst occurs before they respond.

Don't feel threatened by the process of change. List the areas in which you need to make life-enhancing changes, such as giving up drinking, smoking or other bad habits. Evaluate each one to see if you can improve your health by taking certain actions today.

Do your relationships overshadow your beliefs?

In co-dependent relationships, the partners have unrealistic expectations of each other. The relationship becomes all important and you forget what is personally meaningful to you. You don't know what your genuine needs are because you allow the demands of the relationship to supersede your own beliefs.

In any relationship, it's essential to maintain a degree of independence. Recognize the importance of your own beliefs and distinguish your values from your partner's. To have a healthy relationship, you must first have a relationship with yourself so that you know and understand your real needs. Then you can select the qualities that you best appreciate in yourself and share them with another human being.

There's a lot to be gained when you enter a relationship knowing who you are. You know what you can and cannot give to the relationship. You can negotiate your needs and expectations in a realistic way, rather than assume your needs will be met and give your power to the other person. You can maintain your autonomy and avoid the formation of a co-dependent relationship.

Make a list of the important relationships in your life. Identify those in which you cannot be your real self. These are the ones you need to work on.

Do you deny that problems exist?

Throughout history people have had a tendency to ignore their problems. In my family, nobody ever acknowledged openly that anything was wrong. If a relative were to walk around naked in someone else's backyard, they would deny that he was senile. They were completely unwilling to accept that a problem existed. Problems can only be resolved when we get to the root of them. In the 1950s and 1960s, our society remained silent about alcoholism, drug addiction and child abuse in dysfunctional families. We did not encourage people to bring these issues to light. Although we have become more open today, many problems remain hidden. Occupational hazards in the workplace may not be discussed, for example, because management does not want to acknowledge their existence. Rather than risk your livelihood by speaking up, you also deny that the problem exists. It's easier to live with the lies than to fight for change.

Make a list of problems in your professional and personal life that you have not brought to light. You must resolve as many of these as possible to grow. If your problems appear to be insurmountable, then you may need the help of a support group.

Do your associates betray your confidence?

It's painful to learn that someone you confided in has betrayed your trust. Suppose you tell a co-worker or friend that you are looking for a new job, and on your next review the supervisor says, "I understand you're looking for a new job." This breach of trust will make you wary of extending your confidence to anyone. But you shouldn't chastise yourself for having trusted that person. As you become more connected to your intuition, you will be less likely to reveal yourself to untrustworthy people.

Think of an incident when you were betrayed by someone you believed was a friend. Did this experience teach you to pay attention to your intuition?

Are you afraid of reaching your potential?

Sometimes we have great potential but stop just short of realizing it. I have seen people with the makings of great athletes pull back and drop out the moment they started to reach that potential. They realize that once they start on the path to success their lives may never be the same. They're afraid to let go of the familiar, even if it is not right for them, and afraid to face the uncertainty on the road ahead. They anticipate the negative possibilities of change instead of positive ones, such as joy, happiness and new experiences.

The person who can let go of the past and move forward is the one who will find life most rewarding and exciting. Each day can bring something new to life if only you go after it. List the mental and physical roadblocks that prevent your self-expression. What are you afraid to give up? How would your life be more fulfilled if you were to express those things? Make a positive step in that direction, even if it is a small one.

Do you resolve your conflicts?

When you run away from difficulties your whole life will be impaired. Consider the person who never devotes the time needed to bring a project to completion. When the inevitable obstacles arise, he becomes distracted and discouraged and may even quit. By jumping from project to project, and not completing any of them, he is never able to take command of his life.

Your early conditioning may have taught you to avoid difficulties. Perhaps your family tolerated frustrations when things didn't go as anticipated. Can you remain open to new ideas when they don't go as planned, or are you afraid of the unexpected? Are you still trying to please someone else? If your family did not give you unconditional time and attention, if they did not acknowledge your efforts, you may carry a grudge today that stops you from resolving conflicts.

Learning to solve problems and see projects through to completion is a skill that you still can acquire. Make a list of any continuing conflicts in your life and try to resolve them.

Two major factors prevent people from resolving conflicts and moving forward with their lives:

- Believing you're not enough
- Fear

Believing you're not enough

You will limit your growth if you always chastise yourself for not achieving enough. You must learn to be reasonable in your expectations and acknowledge your efforts. Recently I participated in an indoor race at West Point. The man who removed my number after the race said, "It didn't look like you put much effort into that." I ignored him because I had satisfied my criteria for success by completing the race. Even if I had raced slower, in fact, I would have accepted that my effort was complete. Ironically, I later learned that I had broken a national record.

It's important to accept all attempts at growth even if the results are less than perfect. If you only acknowledge the best job possible, you will become stagnant and angered by your own imperfections. Recognize that you cannot improve every single time you try. Life has various plateaus that serve as balancing stages. These plateaus give us time to think about the direction of our lives and get things together. If you reprimand yourself for not advancing, then you will negate much of what you have learned up to that point.

Write about the times that you have chastised yourself for not achieving big results. Think of something positive you have gained from the experience.

Fear

We live in a time of gross uncertainty; nonspecific fears are universal. Since people do not know how to resolve these fears, they blame them on other people or situations around them. They stop themselves from engaging in new activities by rationalizing that they will not like it anyway or that something is bound to go wrong.

Fear and uncertainty can make you feel out of control. An inability to cope is counterproductive to the process of resolving conflicts because it makes you feel depressed and helpless. Then you wait for someone to rescue you. You may form a co-dependent relationship with the first likely candidate to come along. Millions of baby boomers joined cult groups in the 1970s and 1980s because they believed their lives were out of control. They looked to gurus for the answers. They wanted someone else to resolve their conflicts because they did not feel capable of taking on the responsibility themselves.

The same situation can manifest in personal relationships. You act as if you want to fulfill another person's needs but really have a hidden agenda to take care of your own. You might think, "If I use praise or submissiveness as bait to develop a relationship, that person will take care of me." Your neediness compels you to form co-dependent relationships when you fear the challenges of life. You barter away parts of yourself to keep unhealthy relationships alive.

Make a list of the things you feel fearful about. Then make a list of your positive attributes, such as persistence, flexibility and understanding. How can these virtues help you to resolve the conflicts you have listed? Learn to tolerate some uncertainty. You will never be able to control everything, and trying to do so will only make you feel more helpless.

Do you have self-defeating behavior in relationships?

How do you know if you or a potential partner has a tendency toward self-defeating co-dependent behavior? Look for the following signs:

- Having obsessive feelings
- Overreacting
- Dredging up old issues
- Overlooking uniqueness
- Violating boundaries
- Not growing
- Buying into negativity

Having obsessive feelings

You constantly need positive reinforcement because you crave love and attention. When you are excessive you express feelings inappropriately. But no one deserves to be the sole focus of all your psychic energy. It is overwhelming to them and unproductive for you. You must determine what it is that you feel you need so desperately and then begin to understand that need in light of your own psyche. Learn to develop the good and to reject what is not helpful within you.

Overreacting

If you overreact to insignificant events, think about whether your response is unreasonable. You may be resorting to childish emotions to have your demands met. For example, you are so insecure in your relationships that each incident and each statement by the other seems to have enormous significance for your well-being. You must scrutinize everything they say and interrogate them about every nuance of a statement. You cast events in the worst possible light out of a fear that something that might affect your safety will slip by you.

Your overreactions create an environment that feeds rage, anger, frustration and anxiety, and leaves no space for genuine positive feelings. If people do not deal with you in an appropriate way, express honest reactions. But consider the possibility that you have not communicated correctly before you react with inappropriate anger or rage.

Dredging up old issues

You keep dredging up old arguments because you never resolved the issues through honest communications. You're not being honest about the real nature of the problem. You are blaming others for their insensitivity to your needs because you hold them responsible for your nurturing.

Overlooking uniqueness

A person who is not growing generally treats all relationships in the same way. You do not recognize what is unique in a relationship. To understand how dysfunctional this approach is, consider a coach who demands that every athlete train and perform in exactly the same way. He refuses to account for differences in body type, age, bone structure and so forth. It's a terrible way to deal with things. You must learn to respect the individuality of people and relationships.

Violating boundaries

You have no right to invade other people's personal beliefs. But if you are co-dependent, that's the first way in which you will try to influence them.

Not growing

If you focus on immediate problems but overlook their spiritual, emotional and intellectual elements, it's a sure sign that your growth has stagnated. This stagnation indicates that you are out of balance and overly focused on your problems. In fact, the only way that you can resolve problems is to consider them from higher levels.

Buying into negativity

If someone you know always bitches and moans, and you accept what he says or does, then you are supporting co-dependency by participating in the negative behavior. Try not to make excuses for this situation. Just see it for what it is. You don't have to be critical, just honest.

What do you do when things get tough?

When you are under extreme stress—the IRS audits you, you lose your job or you have an interpersonal crisis—you are likely to experience despair and helplessness. You feel out of control, perhaps even nauseous, and try to abandon the situation by seeking the quickest way out. Unfortunately this approach never works because you cannot run away from your problems. What you need to do instead is look for ways to get through crises.

In times such as these, one technique that may prove useful is positive visualization. When I face a conflict, I visualize a long road with a beautiful, beaming, healing light at the end. This image reminds me that the crisis is a part of my spiritual journey. As I travel this path, I notice the dragons and demons of my existence all around me. But rather than focus on them and be consumed by hopelessness and despair, I concentrate on the heroic qualities that will give me the strength to overcome my problems. I think about my virtues that have aided me in the past and present and will support me in the future.

When you pay attention to your best qualities, you will find answers to your problems. When you concentrate on the problem alone, you will remain in crisis. Here are some of the good qualities you need to look for in yourself:

- Love
- Creativity
- Honesty
- Openness
- Trust
- Purpose
- Self-respect
- Sensitivity
- Life-affirming attitude
- Patience and caring
- Self-control
- Spirituality

Love

One of the most positive virtues you can have is an unconditional love of life and love of self. When you need to resolve a crisis or break negative patterns, look at your situation lovingly. Hate will only reinforce the negativity.

Creativity

Creative people have options. You have the ability to express yourself in deeper, more meaningful ways. And you can deal with your problems in new, original ways.

Honesty

Be honest with yourself about the nature of your problem so that you can approach it in a more realistic way.

Openness

You must be open to change, new values and new beliefs. Sometimes a problem signifies that you are holding onto something you need to let go of, such as a relationship that no longer contributes to your growth or your partner's. If you can let go, you may find the answer to your problem.

Trust

Trust that the process of change will be beneficial. Nobody is born a champion, and we all have problems to overcome in life. To get us on the road to change, however, we must trust the process of growth and our own definition of what is important and meaningful.

Purpose

When you have purpose in your life, you will be healthier and better equipped to overcome crises.

Self-respect

Self-respect allows you to react from your needs and intuition, not from a sense of obedience.

Sensitivity

When you are sensitive to yourself, other people and the world around you, your real nature will manifest. Being cruel is the opposite of being sensitive.

Life-affirming attitude

People who take a positive position are inspirations to the world. I think we're all tired of hearing words such as but, can't, won't, shouldn't and couldn't from people who deny life.

Patience and caring

A patient person realizes that the effort needed to accomplish something is worthwhile and that nothing comes all at once. Being caring allows you to empathize with others. People who possess the opposite qualities are restless and uninvolved.

Self-control

You are able to control your own life without tying to manipulate others.

Spirituality

People who recognize a higher power know they are not alone in solving their problems. People who lack a spiritual connection try to resolve their problems in worldly ways with fraud and deception.

To this list of virtues, you could add many others that will help you to break your negative patterns. The more you focus on your assets, the stronger you will become. Becoming strong will make it easier for you to resolve conflicts.

10

If It's My Life, Then Let Me Live It

> *When you are in balance, you will be resolving your fears, acting on your intuitions and desires and feeling satisfied with your life.*

10

What do you want to make important in your life?

Examine the different areas of your life and determine the elements that are important about each. Make a list of those you feel are critical to your well-being. Until you identify these areas and write them down, they may appear to be insignificant. If physical health has meaning to you, write it down. Otherwise, you may miss the connection between wellness and diet and continue to eat too many fatty foods such as hamburgers, pizza or french fries.

Once you decide what is meaningful in each area of life, determine what you must do to act in a way consistent with your priorities. What follows are some areas you might want to consider:

- Relationships
- Financial security
- Spiritual growth
- Sexual fulfillment

- Career growth
- Personal time
- Play time

Relationships

Define the qualities that you want from your relationships. Are your needs different from those you were led to believe are important? Perhaps you associate with the businesspeople rather than the artists you really like because you are expected to mingle with the former. Think about what elements would comprise an ideal relationship for you. You must define what you want from a relationship before you can make it a reality.

Financial security

What does financial security mean to you? To what degree does money—or the lack of it—dictate how you live your life? Some people use a lack of money as an excuse not to live their lives more fully. They may never travel and rarely socialize. And some people who have a lot of money live an equally limited existence. They become overly responsible and never find time for their friends and families. Others with limited incomes lead wonderful, happy lives.

The point is that wealth, in and of itself, is not a determinant of happiness. Why, then, do most people center their lives around money? In large part, they are seeking security. But they may become prisoners to money in the process. For example, many people work at jobs they hate "just for the money." Other people center their lives around money to gain acceptance. Newlyweds, for instance, often rush to buy a home and have a family they cannot afford because their families expect them to. As a result, they go into debt and need to work two jobs.

To avoid the pitfalls of money, you must reassess your material needs. When you want to buy something of significant value, ask what you must sacrifice to own that possession. Is it worth it to you? Can you give it up if you choose to, or will you become too attached to it? Is this something you really want or is it a status symbol that others expect you to own?

Spiritual growth

Is spiritual growth important to you? Are you guided by your conscience or do you live by your animal nature? Do you have real concerns about the world, your fellow man and the quality of life in the world? If your generation and those of the future do not live with and address these concerns, you will suffer for it.

There are people on the streets who have all but eliminated conscience from their daily lives. They lie, steal, cheat, rape and kill without remorse. This sociopathic attitude has become commonplace in all levels of society. Some bankers, corporate raiders and executives do basically the same thing. They are motivated strictly by gratification and are not at all concerned with the consequences of their actions.

Are you complacent about the world, or do you live your life according to a set of principles? Do you address things that you feel are inherently wrong, or do you simply allow them to happen? Are you aware of the quality of energy you put out every time you say, do or think something? Do you contemplate the positive or negative consequences of your actions? To become more fully empowered, you must be the one small voice that speaks out for yourself, your world and the things of value in it.

Sexual fulfillment

Is sexual fulfillment important in your life? Think about the role it plays and the ways in which you can fulfill your needs in a healthy way. If you have a spouse or lover, when was the last time you talked about your real needs in an open, honest way? When is the last time you considered their needs as part of your sexual fulfillment?

Career growth

What are your career aspirations? This time next year, where would you like to be in your career? Have you planned for your professional growth and developed a plan to implement it? Recognize that you will never go anywhere if you do not have a plan and the desire to get there. You won't be able to break through the frustrations and limitations of your present position or profession.

Of course, you can find a million and one excuses to avoid taking the actions that will expand or change the direction of your career. But you could just as easily find a million and one reasons to alter your career. It's all in how you approach it. Excuses such as, "I don't have the time, money and support" are cop-outs that can be turned around and used in your favor. If you lack the proper education for a given career, for example, consider it an opportunity to devise imaginative approaches to the profession. Formal training may give you a set path to follow, but a lack of training will give you original insight into the situation.

Once you achieve the first success, you will identify the next goal you must accomplish. As you climb further up your ladder of success, you will recognize additional goals that are easier to achieve and more rewarding each time you attain one. If you have internal desire, you can do anything. There's nothing you can't do if you start with "I will" rather than "I can't." Don't be discouraged by the time it takes to see results. All things happen in good time if they are worth waiting for, and you shouldn't defer, limit or ignore your goals simply because they take longer to achieve than expected. By focusing your attention on them, you will be able to nurture them to completion with favorable results.

Personal time

Be sure to devote some time solely to your interests. My personal time is important to me because I am continually in the public eye and need time to rebalance. If someone shows up when I need to be alone, I don't hesitate to politely let them know that I will get back to them as soon as I can provide them with my time and attention. I would rather spend a shorter amount of quality time with someone than a longer period during which my attention is diverted by some other need.

Setting aside personal time each day can help to foster your creative, intellectual and spiritual growth. But to do so, you must create boundaries that cannot be crossed. Allowing others to transgress your intellectual and creative boundaries is not without consequences. For example, has anyone ever said to you, "Do you really think that way?" or "You don't really believe that, do you?" That person is showing no respect for your thoughts and feelings. In effect, he or she is saying that you are incapable of making an intellectual judgment on your own.

Most people are never encouraged to develop their own thoughts and beliefs. Early on, parents try to mold their children into who they want them to be instead of allowing them to develop into who they naturally are. In school, students are not supposed to have opinions that differ from their teachers'. Like parrots, they learn to say and do what is acceptable. At the same time, they lose sight of their real thoughts and feelings. This carries over into all phases of adult life. You only do what your doctor says, for example, and dismiss all forms of alternative medicine as quackery.

Unfortunately, children cannot fight back when adults transgress their boundaries or they will be rejected by their families. But you can learn to assert yourself as an adult. When someone asks for your opinion, give it to them in an honest and straightforward manner. This approach affirms what is legitimate for you.

You also need personal time to be creative. It doesn't matter what you create, so long as you receive pleasure from the creation. Many people prevent themselves from creating because they cannot justify the time involved. If it isn't marketable, they say, why devote time to it? As a result, they shut down their creativity. They have been programmed to believe that doing something for the fun of it is a waste of time. But if painting relaxes you and allows you to express yourself, don't let others tell you that it's only worthwhile if you create artwork that can be displayed.

Stop thinking that you must justify your actions and your mode of expression to anyone. Nobody's judgment should deter you from your creative outlets. The value of engaging in any particular activity comes from your inner perspective.

Play time

Like most people, you probably do not give play time much credence. You take life too seriously. You get into heavy relationships and serious situations. You think play is something children do and grown-ups have no time for. In reality, life can be fun at any age. By allowing yourself time to play you lighten your load and keep your life in balance. Associate with people who understand that play is an important part of relationships. Lighten up. Have some fun with life.

What do you plan to do to change your life?

You've decided what is important to you and where you need to modify your life. Now you need a system to implement the necessary changes. Otherwise, change is simply not going to happen. You will see glimpses of what you want to change rolling through in your mind but you will never do anything about it.

Using all the lists you have developed here as a guide, make a schedule that allows time to concentrate on all the important areas of your life. Focus on the actions that will turn your life around in a positive direction. How can you use these times to your best advantage? What are the first steps you need to take to refocus your life? Don't feel that the first schedule you make is the one you must live with for the rest of your life. You can modify it as your life patterns change and continue to concentrate on the areas that will empower you.

What beliefs limit your growth?

As difficult as it may be, you may need to modify your beliefs to create positive change in your life. Take an honest look at your current beliefs. Which ones limit you, and what defense mechanisms do you use to hold on to them? Are you willing to do what it takes to let go of these beliefs? This is a difficult exercise because everyone tends to surround themselves with people and things that reinforce their beliefs—their parents, religion, school, job and friends.

Sometimes you need to get away from familiar surroundings to gain a new perspective of your beliefs. One person who joined my detoxification program told me that being with our group helped him modify his beliefs and eliminate negative people from his life. Previously, he had always made excuses for their behaviors and attitudes. Now he can relate to more positive people. But he had to get out of his environment to see the situation objectively.

Your environment and the people in it may be healthy, positive and nurturing, or they may not. Be honest in your assessment and see your surroundings for what they are. Don't condemn or try to change what you cannot. You must respect others' rights to live as they see fit. To change your own life and belief systems, however, you must carefully examine them to see what works and what does not.

Do you express your autonomy?

Autonomy is crucial to growth, and yet many people fear it. They don't want to stand out from the crowd and believe they must live their lives in an average way to be acceptable to others. Living to please others is pointless. No matter what you do, some people will support your efforts and some will not. People see things from different perspectives because they come from dissimilar backgrounds. Therefore, their attitudes and beliefs might be right for them but wrong for you.

Granted, it is difficult to be autonomous in a society that

values homogeny. Children are taught to think and behave in the same way. Those who think and feel differently from the group run the risk of being ridiculed. This also happens to people in the health movement. One day when I talked about my book, *Good Food, Good Mood*, on my radio show, a man called in and said, "I'm not one of those 'health food nuts' but I'm getting more fiber in my diet." He couldn't just admit that he felt good about the changes he was making. Instead, he had to show his friends that he was still a part of their group.

People distance themselves from anything that appears to be extreme. And in our society, doing something that announces to the world that you are an independent person is extreme. Living in a nontoxic environment is extreme. Detoxifying the pollutants from your body is extreme. But that doesn't mean you should not pursue these goals by being an autonomous individual.

Make a list of the ways in which you would like to express your autonomy. What would you like to do that is meaningful to you but appears extreme to others?

Do you accept responsibility for too many things?

Make a list of all your responsibilities and then prioritize them so that the most important ones will receive the most time and attention. Accept that you have certain responsibilities that you cannot change. But also look to see if you have taken on responsibilities that are not necessary or beneficial to you. If you spend time agonizing over things that you do not need to be responsible for, you will not have time to make beneficial and meaningful changes in your life. You should be responsible, but you should choose what you will be responsible for.

Do you do the things that give your life meaning?

Make a list of the things you do for the simple joy of doing them. If you jog each morning, for example, you may feel tired and achy but you've also accomplished your goal of enhancing your health. If at the end of the day you haven't put any garbage food into your body, you've made a positive step toward better health. If you do things for others but expect nothing in return, you've helped society and also rewarded yourself. When I jog in the park and find a rock or a stick in my path, for example, I always remove it so that other people won't have to contend with the hazard. It's not important to be acknowledged for such acts; the self-satisfaction of helping others is reward enough.

You must respect yourself before you can respect others. Respect for yourself, others and the world around you is what makes life meaningful. Don't procrastinate about doing the things that are meaningful to you. Don't put off a vacation because you don't have the time or money, and don't put off a relationship because you are too busy working. You will limit your existence if you play these games with yourself. You need to live your life every day in a meaningful way. Life is much too precious to not live it to the fullest.

Are unreasonable fears holding you back?

The following fears often are used to justify a lack of progress in life: taking a chance, competition, autonomy, intimacy, letting go, being open, being criticized, being unaccepted, losing control. Make a list of your fears and work to eliminate the ones that are holding you back.

When you make a change that you originally feared, you typically find that your fear was an illusion and that the dreaded results never materialized. Perhaps you need to change some aspect of your job, such as working new hours or taking a longer lunch, but you're afraid to approach your boss. Really, the worst thing that can happen is that he will say no. But if you prepare yourself well, you can show the boss that the change will not affect your work or productivity. You'll be happier and he will benefit from your continued productivity.

As this example shows, you must concentrate on the good that can result from change, not from the fears that deter you. When I lecture on natural health to a group of medical students, I fully realize that many people in the room will not accept the things that I am telling them. In fact, many will be angry with me. But the benefits of having even one person respond favorably to my lecture eliminates any apprehension I may feel. When you act on the things you fear, you become more empowered with each success and your unreasonable fears will begin to dissipate.

What other things are holding you back?

In addition to unreasonable fears, consider what other attitudes, behavioral patterns and physical constraints are holding you back from making positive change. These may include the following:

- Home
- Food
- Addictions
- Blocked communication
- Burdensome priorities
- Isolation
- Overresponsibility
- Too much restraint
- Lack of curiosity
- No sense of adventure
- Overlooking opportunities
- Unhealthy competition
- No relaxation
- Insecurity
- Avoidance of conflict
- Unrealistic goals
- Barriers
- Limits
- Materialistic values
- Irrelevant rules
- Lack of support
- Failure
- Holding back

Home

Does most of your time, money and attention go toward owning and maintaining a home? Has it become the driving force in your life, causing you to sacrifice other important goals? If so, step back and see if your home has become an obsession. If it's taking most of your time and energy, perhaps you would be better off renting.

Food

What role does food play in your life? Do you live to eat or eat to live? Your food should be dedicated to making you healthier. It should be enjoyable to eat but not a pastime or an obsession. What modifications do you need to make to eat better and obtain a healthier lifestyle?

Addictions

What addictions do you need to clear out of your life? Typical ones include cigarettes, coffee, food, alcohol, relationships, sex and work.

Blocked Communication

Are you willing to communicate openly? Can you be honest about your needs? Can you allow people to see the real you instead of the one they have grown accustomed to? You'll have to prepare others for the fact that you're changing. Tell them that you are committed to making changes in your life and that you would like them to recognize the true you instead of the imitation. Let them know what the real you will be, without being intimidating or apologetic.

As you make changes, notice whether or not they accept you for who you are. You will want to maintain a relationship with the ones who do; the others may need to go by the wayside. Remember, too, that communication is the most important aspect of any relationship, and the changes you make may very well alter the nature of your communication. If you have been dominant, you may begin to listen more. If you have been submissive, you may become more dominant and speak up for yourself.

Burdensome priorities

Priorities are the parts of your life to which you devote specific blocks of time and attention. Make a list of your current priorities. Do you do these things by choice or because you are expected to? Are you willing to establish healthy priorities and rid yourself of unhealthy ones? The most difficult priorities to release are those that stroke your self-esteem, such as sending your child to an expensive school you cannot afford or working two jobs to finance your materialistic success. But some priorities are burdens that you must lift to live more fully. Other people may say you are being irresponsible, but your first responsibility is to yourself. Any priorities driven by guilt need to be eliminated from your life.

Isolation

Do you isolate yourself from the events around you, or do stay abreast of what's happening in the world? As social creatures, we don't live in a vacuum. We are a product of our environment, and everybody has a subtle influence on the world. Life will not go on as usual because you are complacent; rather, your complacency will allow others to gain a controlling influence that may not be in your best interests.

How can you be more aware of and involved in critical issues, such as the environment, human rights and animal rights? Choose the ones that are important to you and resolve to make a difference. Even if you don't join a formal organization to express your interest in an issue, you can influence others through the sincerity of your conversations on the issues that have meaning for you.

Overresponsibility

Do you express your independence or are you tied to your relationships and responsibilities? I once went on a trip with a friend who felt he had to call home every few hours. It was obvious to me that he was more involved in the events of his home life than in enjoying himself on the trip. Sometimes you just need to let go and get away.

Can you get away from your everyday life? Can you enjoy an occasional retreat from your familiar surroundings?

Too much restraint

What do you do to show spontaneity? Do you ever do anything on the spur of the moment? Do you climb a mountain just because it's there? Do you take a day off from work and drive to the country?

Make a list of the things you do that are uniquely yours. What sets you apart from other people? Do you dress in an original way or have original ideas? Do you do anything that is absolutely different?

Lack of curiosity

Are you curious about life and nature? Do you enjoy learning new things just for the sake of learning? As children we have a natural curiosity that is unblemished by ulterior motives. But as adults we allow our curiosity to be overshadowed by the mundane aspects of life. Before we know it, we have lost sight of our learning abilities and become stagnant and complacent. Eventually, we channel all of our efforts into making money and doing what's expected of us. We no longer take the time to explore life.

Average adults allow their curiosity to be satisfied by short, canned experiences, such as watching television or going to the movies. Or perhaps we accumulate knowledge for the purpose of display. Few adults take the time to satisfy their curiosity with a nature walk, a trip to a museum or even a good book. What do you do every day to express your curiosity?

No sense of adventure

How often do you head out into the unknown, without a clear idea of what will happen? Without some adventure in your life, you will become a boring person. Many people go on Freedom Bound Journeys, where they rough it for a week and forego their creature comforts. Despite the lack of any modern conveniences, they return from the adventure feeling exhilarated. Do you have any adventure in your life?

Overlooking opportunities

Do you seize opportunities when they present themselves? Or do you sit around and wait for opportunity to knock? If you let new adventures in life pass you by without responding, you will no doubt regret it. Most people don't take the time and energy to create their own opportunities. They want the opportunities to come to them. But if you don't work to create opportunities, then you normally don't have the motivation to take advantage of them when they do arise. You miss out on a lot of life's excitement.

Unhealthy competition

Unhealthy competition stunts personal growth; healthy competition enhances it. Competition is healthy when you relate to your own past accomplishments, rather than go head to head with someone else. When I race I don't compete against anyone else on the track. I compete with myself to try to do better each time. Sometimes I enter races knowing that I don't have a chance to win because I will be racing with Olympic champions. I enter for my own satisfaction. Racing with such people—and having my time logged in an official record—motivates me to beat my previous time.

No relaxation

People who must occupy their minds at all times do not know how to relax. It's important to take the time to mellow out each day and eliminate the tensions of life. You can't do this by watching television, reading a book or otherwise occupying your mind. You need to let your mind relax after a hard day, just as you let your body relax after physical exercise.

Insecurity

Be secure in and of yourself. Don't rely on unnatural, manmade security to make you feel good about who you are. In today's workplace, which is rife with cutbacks and layoffs, people have learned that they can no longer rely on the outside sense of security that provided workers before them with a sense of protection.

Clearly, true security comes from within. When you live out your values and feel satisfied with your relationships, you will be secure. Recently I talked to a woman working at a healthfood store in a small artists' community in New Mexico. When I asked her what she did prior to moving there, she said she had been a corporate lawyer. She had become disenchanted with the rules and regulations laid down by authority and went to New Mexico to do what she wanted and be who she was.

For her, financial security, job security and relationship security were not as important as being with herself. The way in which you view security determines what you will do with your life.

Avoidance of conflict

How do you handle conflict? Do you view it as an opportunity to grow, or do you run away and hope that the conflict will resolve itself? If you're intimidated by conflict, you will not grow. The same conflict will simply reappear in your life. Think about whether you are resolving your conflicts.

Unrealistic goals

Have you always set goals for yourself? If so, evaluate them to see if they are healthy, positive and realistic.

Barriers

How do you view things that seem to stand in your way? Do you give up immediately and use the barrier as an excuse not to continue, or do you view it as a challenge and resolve to meet it head on?

Limits

Do you recognize that many of the things limiting your growth are artificial and can be overcome? You can motivate yourself to transcend any situation.

Materialistic values

Examine your values to determine if they are superfluous. Do you impose artificial limits on your social life by associating only with people of a certain social status, economic level or education? Do you value material existence more than nature?

Look at all the people and experiences you are missing out on in life by subscribing to these values.

Irrelevant rules

Is your life controlled by rules and regulations? Take a hard look at your sense of independence. Is it limited by all the things you are expected to do?

Lack of support

If you do not get real support from your friends and family, it may be time to devote more energy to people who will support your efforts to grow and change. Real support is unconditional, while the support we get from most people is shallow and self-interested. Most people don't want to see you change because they are not ready to change themselves. A drinking buddy will not want you to quit drinking, for example, because then you will not have anything in common. You must give up certain relationships and look for more supportive ones.

Failure

Your failures should serve as learning experiences, not measures of inadequacy. No experience is a true failure if you learn from it in ways you did not anticipate. These beneficial lessons ultimately aid the process of growth. When you try something and fail, you may learn that you are not really cut out for that area and need to channel your energies into other endeavors. Equally important, failure can be a time of reassessment. Perhaps your presentation or audience was wrong in a new business venture, and you can now approach the goal in a different manner. As long as you are afraid of failure, you will never take chances and you will never grow.

Holding back

When you have an idea, do you actualize it or ignore it? Do you have the confidence to share your ideas with a support group? Better yet, do you have a support group that allows you to share your ideas without ridicule? You need to share your ideas with people who help you make them happen. If the people who support you cannot help you directly, they may lead you to the right people to make your ideas materialize. When you have faith in your ideas, you will find creative ways to overcome the obstacles that limit most people.

Do you try to reduce your negativity?

Negative attitudes can make you feel disempowered, helpless and controlled by others. Make a list of things you were negative about today. Think of ways you could have turned these events or feelings into positive situations. Try to visualize the end results.

Do you have a purpose in your life?

Having a purpose in life gives you direction and allows you to focus your time and talents on your goals. Without a purpose, you will wander aimlessly through life, dissipating your energies without accomplishing meaningful goals. Be aware that you may need to change your purpose as you grow. The important point is to maintain a clear view of what you want to accomplish so that your efforts will be concentrated.

If your purpose in life is unclear, make a list of things that are important to you and things that you like to do. Use these as a guide to help you find your purpose.

How can you modify your behavior?

Once you identify behaviors you want to change, you must trace the roots of these behavior patterns. Otherwise, you will continue to perpetuate the same old behaviors over and over and nothing will change. When you trace a behavior to its roots, it becomes easier to let it go. And, of course, any behavior that adversely affects your mental or physical health should be at the top of the list of those you want to modify, such as smoking, drugs, alcohol, eating habits, anger, violence and stress.

Are you overlooking certain realities?

Most of us only examine the beliefs presented to us by our religion, school, parents, friends and work. But some of these beliefs limit your ability to find solutions to problems. It's important to examine other beliefs with an open mind. In the 1960s, for example, many people went outside the Western culture to examine Eastern religion. This willingness to explore other ideas gave them new insight into the meaning of life.

When you have an open mind and a spirit of adventure, you may discover hidden ideas, beliefs, values and solutions in places you otherwise would not have looked.

What things do you purposely avoid?

No doubt you have certain goals in life that you always find an excuse not to pursue. Make a list of these, since identifying them is the first step to facing them. Be sure to include everything you avoid in the major areas of your life, such as your career, your relationships and your family. This exercise allows you to focus on the ones that are important to your growth and fulfillment. It also helps you to clarify any concepts in your life that are ill-defined and therefore difficult to modify.

What parts of your life are out of balance?

Put the various elements of your life into proportion, according to the real value they have for you. Your work and your pleasure each must have its own time and place. When your life is in balance, you will be satisfied with the way everything is going. You will be happy with your work, for example, rather than doing a job you dislike or wanting to make a transition to a new job.

For practical purposes, balance can be defined as a state in which everything that can be dealt with has been dealt with. There are no festering problems nor unresolved questions lingering in your mind. There are no inner conflicts that gnaw away at you. In essence, your life is in order: You are eating the right foods, doing the right exercises on a routine basis, talking out your problems, resolving your fears and acting on your intuitions and desires.

When you concentrate on one area of your life, the others do not interfere with the tasks or pleasures at hand.

Conversely an imbalance in any area of your life will carry

over into everything else you do. When unresolved problems cannot be set aside, your mind will not be on the task at hand. Thus, you cannot forget about your work problems when you are at home with your family, or your work suffers because of unresolved problems at home.

For this reason, you need to deal with unresolved conflicts as they arise. At the very least, get them out in the open so that you can acknowledge they exist and need to be resolved. This approach will allow you to focus your time and attention on one area, without dissipating your energies in other parts of your life. Maintaining this essential balance is one of the keys to a better life.

Rediscovering Your Real Self

> To be a healthier person,
> value your uniqueness and
> look for the people in the
> world who will accept you
> just the way you are.

11

Do your parents expect you to live out their dreams?

How do your parents respond when you pursue your ideals? Do they support your efforts to express these ideals, or do they burst your bubble and dictate how you should live? Suppose your father expects you to be a football star because he never reached the big time himself and sees you as his proxy ego. But you would like to be a pianist because music expresses your artistic nature. If your father verbalizes his disapproval of this "unmasculine" choice, he denies your real needs.

The question is, do you need your father's opinion to reaffirm that you are okay? If so, you will deny yourself the satisfaction of doing something meaningful and try to live for him instead. You may even be successful at it, but you will never be fulfilled because it is his dream, not yours. The same is true of women, of course, who often make choices to gain their parents' approval. Men and women alike must curb the tendency to live through their parents' egos.

Be honest in looking at all areas of your life. Have the

courage to see what is before your eyes. You will destroy your instinctual and intuitive self if you do not let yourself know what you know. Anything you do not want to see is the very thing you need to see. You will become curious about many things when you stop narrowing your reality through denial of what is painful to you. When you question your conditioning, you will free yourself. When you eliminate negativity from your life, you will find your creativity.

Are your relationships dysfunctional?

Tell other people the truth about yourself; otherwise, you will encourage dysfunctional relationships. You must be able to define your real needs and express them to others. Your relationships should acknowledge and honor those needs. Why choose to stay in any relationship—be it with a lover, family member, friend or job—if your needs are not addressed? If the relationship only allows you to recognize artificial or socially contrived needs, you will be completely unfulfilled.

The longer you display false happiness, the more you feed a dysfunctional relationship. If someone tells you repeatedly that your thoughts are wrong or stupid, he is transgressing your intellectual and emotional boundaries. And if you allow yourself to be invalidated this way, you will only have merit when someone of importance agrees with you. This process fuels insecurity, which will cause you to look and listen very carefully to see how other people view reality. With no reality of your own, you will try to match your actions to their reality so that they will continue to accept you. But the moment you go against anyone else's views or beliefs, you are discounted.

Are you conditioned to condone injustice?

Government, industry, religion and other institutions exert an enormous amount of control over people. In all walks of life, we see examples of what happens to those who voice a challenge to authority. Consider the Amish woman who quietly challenged the subservient role of women in the Amish religion. She said that women should have the right to join in the governing process. What did she get for her efforts? She was reprimanded by the church and then excommunicated when she persisted. Her husband divorced her and her children were brainwashed to abandon her. The church's influence was so strong that every single friend and family member turned against her. But what had she really done to deserve such harsh treatment?

For another example of the injustices spawned by institutions, one need only look at organized medicine. Patients who choose a nontraditional approach to treatment, such as nutrition or vitamin therapy, are considered to be irrational by society at large. And the doctors who offer these treatments are branded as quacks. The controlling boards of the medical establishment do not hesitate to punish doctors who do not abide by their standards.

No matter that the doctor is healing patients. He or she will pay for traveling an alternative path. One doctor in California, for example, offered nutritional therapy to cancer patients who had not been helped by radiation or chemotherapy, the mainstays of conventional medicine. He helped more than 260 patients strengthen their immune system and overall health without the side effects of conventional therapy.

What did he get for his efforts? Marshals broke into his

house and arrested him and his wife. Later he was convicted of a felony, but not because his patients were dying or his method was scientifically unacceptable. In fact medical literature supports the efficacy of nutritional therapy. And it was not because his colleagues did not support him. Many people came forward to testify that his treatment made sense.

He was convicted and sentenced to hard labor for one reason alone: He went against the institutional grain and chose something different. He rejected the prescribed treatment of chemotherapy, surgery and radiation, none of which truly help to heal cancer patients. The laws of California favor the medical monopoly so overwhelmingly that anyone who steps over the line, no matter how well they succeed, will be destroyed. Any doctor who has deviated since also has been destroyed.

Isn't it strange that no one from the church, the media or the political and educational communities came forth to intervene on this doctor's behalf? They did not say, "This doctor is treating people and they're getting well. We're crucifying him for it. That doesn't make sense." Here again, the established system we have been conditioned to accept simply does not face any challenge.

In fact, our conditioning teaches us to accept the many contradictions, inconsistencies and failures within our belief systems. We resign ourselves to living within the system and silence the objections raised by our mind and spirit. We fail to recognize that our social systems are based on pure economics, and we don't question whether industry has the people's interests at heart, which it clearly does not. If society tells us to live and eat in ways that produce disease, we become prisoners of disease. If the meat industry tells us to eat cancer-causing meat, we deny this cause-and-effect relationship because we have been brainwashed to believe that meat is healthy.

The paradigms set forth by society are powerful forces indeed. Trying to change them can be like trying to move a mountain. Even so, you can take small steps that will eventually change an unjust system. First and foremost, you must redirect your energies from unjust systems to those that support your beliefs. You can buy household products that do not use animals in their testing and invest in companies that do not violate human rights. You can encourage healthier farming practices by buying organic food. As more and more people take such actions, small change becomes a trend, which, in turn, becomes the norm. New paradigms are created through the process of enlightenment.

Make a list of the things you truly believe in. Are you supporting these beliefs with your time and money?

Do you waste time in relationships that prevent you from growing?

In all likelihood, the patterns of healthy and unhealthy behavior that you learned in childhood are with you today. But remember the first rule of empowerment: You don't have to justify anything to anyone at any time when you are on your own. You don't have to consult with, share with, or get approval from your family. It's your life. You can live it as you wish.

Our families condition us to be obedient for so long that we continue to seek their approval throughout life. You probably know the routine: You take a boyfriend or girlfriend home to get the family's approval. Who's marrying the person anyway, you or your family? When you want to change jobs, move or start a new career, you consult with your family to make sure the change will be accepted. Why? It's your life, not theirs. This is not to say, of course, that you shouldn't share growth and happiness with your family, provided they are supportive of your ideas. In that case, they will see that you are taking positive steps toward personal growth. They will help you in your decision-making process and you will benefit from that support.

But if the love you received was conditional, a sense of fear will haunt you for the rest of your life. You will fear abandonment, which makes us feel that we are alone, unlovable and unworthy. You'll spend your whole life trying to make someone else love you. You may overwork and overstrive. Spontaneity will fade from your life because you cannot release the child in you, whom you believe to be unacceptable. In the end, everything you do will be aimed at making others feel comfortable with you. You will act like a compliant child no matter how old you get. It's just a game, but a vicious one indeed.

To be a healthier person, you must stop the game. You don't have to be obedient to anyone, nor must you alter your nature to gain the acceptance of others. There are people in the world who will accept you just as you are. Look for them.

Make a list of all your important relationships and evaluate whether or not they are healthy. Are the others supportive of your beliefs or do they try to influence you with their own?

How do you deal with stress?

There's no denying that today's society produces enormous stress. The sad part, however, is that we have very few healthy mechanisms for alleviating that stress. The average American, with too many unpaid bills, may try to release stress by watching Gladiators on Saturday afternoon. The announcer gets them worked up at the prospect of watching a tractor roll over other cars. What does that say about our coping mechanisms? Does it really resolve stress to watch someone crush the top of six cars in eight seconds?

The strange methods of relaxation adopted by our culture show no appreciation of the higher values in life, such as spirituality, intellect and creativity. Instead, society encourages us to form addictive habits, supposedly to alleviate tension, when in fact they compound the stress. For decades, movies and television commercials influenced people to smoke, drink and take prescription drugs to relieve daily stress. To this day, good health habits and whole, healthy meals are not depicted. If all you ever see are people who drink coffee on the run, you will revert to this image when trying to subdue stress. I'd much rather watch an 80-year-old woman skate at Laguna Beach or see a 90-year-old man run a marathon. That, to me, is normal. The hippies of the 1960s also showed us how to have fun with life and to express ourselves with bright colors, dance and music. For the most part, their attitude about life was a healthy reaction to their parents' disapproval of fun. Their nonsmiling, serious parents never let them forget the sacrifices they had made for them. They expected their children to become just as obedient, contrived, controlled and powerless as they were— the perfect prescription for passing on stress-related diseases to the next generation.

America's addictions manifest in our powerless attitudes, our lack of bonding and honesty and our inability to actualize life. We tend to overlook the real values and seek instead a false utopia. We want to escape the everyday monotony and boring routines of our lives. Therefore we look for something to distract us from the seemingly unchangeable nature of our lives. Coffee, alcohol, cigarettes, cocaine, marijuana and crack—all of these appear to give us the high that will take away the pain for a moment.

We turn to drugs when we don't feel good about who we are and when we are not encouraged to engage in life. The kid on the street taking crack, the adult on Wall Street taking cocaine and the politician sidling up to the bar have one thing in common. They're all in pain. But rather than be honest about the cause of the pain, we blame others for our addictions—the South American coke dealers, the cigarette manufacturers, the bars that serve alcoholics. The truth is that if we put every cocaine dealer in the world in jail, coke would be back on the streets in six months.

A crisis cannot be resolved by addressing the symptoms alone; you have to dig deeper to get to the cause. But that would mean acknowledging that your guiding paradigm is flawed. As a nation, we don't want to admit that our biases, prejudices and lazy thinking are erroneous. It's too painful. Instead we choose to blame others for our problems, pointing the finger at anyone who is not a part of us. This hostility leads us to create artificial, unnecessary conflicts in the world.

Ultimately we end up with misdirected, stressful lives. We try to relate to other people through soap operas, trashy novels and magazines, movies and even the evening news. Why would you be interested in someone else's sex life? Perhaps you don't have one of your own. Why would you be interested in someone else's success? Perhaps you don't feel successful in life. What do you gain from soap operas, which are filled with treachery, adultery, murder, deceit and lies? That's not real life.

Participating in someone else's pain and discomfort may allow you to escape from your own feelings, but it's a negative way to deal with stress. People who are living their own lives don't have the time or the inclination to worry about how other people live.

And what about the news? Every evening, we see that people have been murdered, burned in car wrecks and so on. Will this make you feel good and enhance your life? We should be reading books or watching shows that provide insight and information and contribute to our growth. No wonder so many people are dysfunctional since we receive so little input on being functional.

What causes stress in your life?

To deal with stress effectively, you must identify stress-generators in your life. Some of the common ones include:

- Family
- Personal environment
- Career
- Relationship
- Self

Family

Families can create stress by transgressing the boundaries of their members, assuming that they have a right to do or say anything they want to another family member without respect for his or her feelings. Stress also is created when a family member is inflexible, impatient and unwilling to listen and learn. You must deal with such stress as soon as it arises.

What's more, you may not spend enough quality time with your family because you don't make the time or you devote too much time to matters of less importance. Ideally, much of your time should be spent with family, friends and yourself. If you're spending it elsewhere, you are allowing superficial needs to overshadow essential ones.

Make a list of the stresses in your family life. These are the ones you need to change.

Personal environment

Your environment may be stressful if it's too small, too large, too noisy, too hard to maintain or too costly. Have you ever said to yourself, "I could enjoy life more if I didn't have the stress of maintaining this expensive house or lifestyle?" You may fool yourself into believing you will enjoy yourself once the house is paid off or the kids are gone. But that day never seems to come.

Sometimes the only solution is to let go. If your house is a true burden, consider getting rid of it. This can be a real challenge if you have a large emotional investment in the house. To ease the transition, visualize the advantages of living in a place you can afford. In other cases, you may need to get away from your immediate surroundings to determine whether or not they are healthy for you. You may discover that your present environment is satisfactory after all or that it needs to be changed.

I once met a man in a small New England town who had returned to the town following a stint in the Midwest. He had moved away to work as a computer scientist, but eventually realized that his 15-hour workdays did not allow room for him to have a life. With that awareness, he made the decision to return to his roots and live a more balanced life. The desire to return had been in the back of his mind for some time, but it was his time away that made him appreciate what he originally had.

When he came home, he bought an old house and spent much of his time fixing it up. He was able to relax because he could easily afford the house and didn't have to devote so much time to work. And he was able to spend more time with his family, his friends and himself. He earned only one-tenth of his former salary, he said, but his life was a hundred times better.

That's going home in the right way. Your essential needs really have nothing to do with the things you are conditioned to want. All across America, people are returning home with this attitude, but not necessarily to the home they came from. They are going to environments that feel like home and make them comfortable. If you don't feel that you belong in your environment, you will feel out of place in everything you do.

I meet many people in my travels who tell me they can never commit themselves to anything because they don't feel comfortable with their situation. As a result, they always have one foot out the door in their relationships, their work and every phase of their lives. These people are always confused, always in crisis. They can never give their full energy to anything or anyone.

List the things you cannot afford in terms of time and money. Assess their importance to determine which you might be better off without. Then list the aspects of your environment that make you feel comfortable or uncomfortable. Do you have a burning desire to live in a different sort of environment, or are you happy where you are? To perform this analysis, learn more about other parts of the country that interest you.

Career

Is your career too limiting, competitive or demanding? Does it just not feel right? If your career is in crisis, whatever the reason, you must address the cause of that stress. Identify the conditions behind these feelings; then, either change the conditions or change your career.

To get to the root of your problem, listen to your inner guides. They are in touch with your intuitive feelings and thus will give you good guidance. All you need then is the courage to follow through on your decision. I meet men and women across America who are starting over in their careers—and feeling much better for it. They undergo some tremendous changes, but the process allows them to live in a more enjoyable, stress-free way.

Make a list of the aspects of your career that concern you. Can you change these things, or do you need to change your career entirely?

Relationships

If you accept the traditional paradigm, which teaches us to feel threatened by anyone who is different, then your relationships will be stressful. How many people have you rejected in your life without knowing why? Do you look for excuses or minor flaws in others to justify your inclination not to socialize with them?

It's not an unusual tactic. Take a look around. You never see the rich with the poor, the educated with the uneducated, the beautiful with the ugly, the healthy with the sick. That's because people feel threatened outside of their narrowly defined categories. If they have difficulty listening to their instincts, they also may have trouble determining who is safe. To broaden your life, you must accept different realities and respect people for who they are. If you show your respect in a noncompetitive way, you will have the opportunity to learn from people of all types.

The imbalances in relationships can create stress as well. You may be too dominant or overly submissive. Your relationship may be too sexual or not sexual enough. You may be giving too much time to the relationship or taking it for granted. You may feel jealous or you may provoke jealousy in your mate.

Whatever the imbalance, you can only solve such problems by identifying the issues at hand and getting them out in the open. If you cannot be honest about your real needs and feelings, nothing will change. Don't worry if you are initially afraid to talk about the problems. Once you start, you may find that the process enhances the relationship. When you bring your feelings to light, you may even find that the other person thinks and feels the same way. If you cannot talk your problems out, it may be time to let the relationship go.

Make a list of the relationships you have now and the ones you would like to have. Evaluate the ones that could be most beneficial to you and nurture these relationships.

Self

With a balanced life, you have time for your body, mind, spirit and emotions. Those who lack this balance may throw all their energy in one direction, to the exclusion of all else, or they may scatter their energy among too many areas.

If you are not careful, you can easily overcommit yourself.

Learn to say yes when you mean yes and no when you mean no. Have the self-assurance to know that you can give an honest response. You may find that the only time you are truly honest is when you yell in anger; otherwise you conceal the truth behind hidden agendas. Wouldn't it be better to be happy and honest?

To eliminate stress, you must be consistent in your life. It doesn't pay to go overboard in one direction or the other. Many people experience too many swings in their lives: They become too lonely or too excited, they need someone or they become aloof, they can't express themselves at all or they overreact. To end these gyrations, establish balance and focus on healthy endeavors. Allow yourself to heal by taking the time to play every day, not just on weekends or holidays.

What first step are you willing to take to initiate change?

Decide today to change something in your life, and then take a first step toward making that change. What first step do you feel comfortable taking? Don't worry if it is not the best or most appropriate step. Don't let an imperfect step stop you from taking any action at all. Just begin. Take the first step.

Consider this example: A person with a kind nature, who tends to be taken advantage of by certain people, decides to become more assertive and confront these people. He has identified the change he wants to make, but he may not be certain what to do when the situation next arises. The important part is that he has resolved to assert himself. As a first step, he may read a book on the topic or join a support group to help him overcome his doubts and fears.

In time, your small successes will build your confidence in making important changes. You will be using a challenging situation to change, grow and express your true nature. List the areas in which you need, to change, and commit to taking a first step, whether alone or with the help of a support group.

What do you do that is boring, meaningless and unfulfilling?

These activities will disempower you and rob your life of excitement and spontaneity. Human beings are social by nature, but that does not mean you must lose your uniqueness to exist in a larger society. You are free to be original and spontaneous as long as you show respect for other people's values.

Write about the areas of your life that you find boring, meaningless and unfulfilling. Which would you like to eliminate? What would you like to do instead? Think about how you can express your uniqueness and, in the process, give your life more essential meaning.

What types of people do you look up to?

Frequently the very qualities you admire in others are the ones you yearn to express yourself. In people you look up to, you see an essential part of yourself that you were never encouraged to develop. Suppose that you were once excited by the idea of a spiritual journey and you meet a man who has been on a spiritual path for some time. You admire him for having persevered and attained great peace and insight. In your own life, you had done more "practical" things by taking a job, marrying and having children. As the years passed, you felt more and more bound by your responsibilities. Now your encounter with this man reminds you of a part of yourself that you had almost forgotten. You wonder if pursuing a spiritual path would bring greater happiness to your life.

Pay attention to the qualities you admire in others. Identify the people you look up to and the characteristics in them that you respect. Ask yourself, do I need to express these qualities in myself? No one else can complete your development for you, and an awareness of the qualities you admire in others can be key to understanding your own needs.

What purpose do your work and relationships serve?

Ask yourself what you are truly striving for in your work and relationships. Is the work you do essential to your life, or do you work for financial rewards only? Are you in an ideal relationship, but somehow you and your partner do not work toward personal ideals? Reevaluate the essence and purpose of your work and relationships. Perhaps they have gotten off track.

Beyond that, define the roles of the important people in your life. What do these people mean to you? This process may enlighten you about the reasons behind your relationships. And it will help you to evaluate whether these people should or should not remain a part of your life.

How do you express love, intimacy, vulnerability, anger, pain, hope and other emotions? With whom do you share your feelings?

The emotions you feel comfortable expressing may depend on who you are with. For example, you may be able to express love and intimacy, but not negative emotions, with your partner. Instead you feel more comfortable sharing any fear and insecurity about the relationship with a close friend. Consequently your friends know more about how you feel toward your partner than he or she does. That makes for incomplete communication within the relationship.

Identify any feelings that go unexpressed in your relationships and address these incomplete emotions. Perhaps you and your partner could write a poem to each other expressing your feelings in a constructive way. You can express more through verse and rhyme than through talking because you must break down your thoughts and feelings to write a poem. In conversation, by contrast, you may rationalize your feelings away and generalize your thoughts and spoken words.

This is a particularly good exercise for men because they tend to hide their feelings. Women, on the other hand, are usually more connected to their emotions.

Write a poem or story about the unlearned lessons of your childhood, young adulthood or adulthood.

By writing about the unfinished lessons of your childhood, you can help put your past behind you. This exercise may take months, but it is well worth the effort. To start, sit down quietly and recall the past. As you look at your life, see the lessons that you never had a chance to complete. If you are like most people, past circumstances have limited your potential for growth. And the older you get, the more difficult change may be. If you can find out what is missing in your life, you can open yourself up to greater fulfillment.

Imagine how your life would be different had you completed these unlearned lessons. Let's say that you were musically inclined as a child but never given the opportunity to take music lessons. As an adult you have lost touch with that creative part of yourself. By rekindling this desire through visualization, you may be able to incorporate the talent into your life once more. You may not be the professional musician you once could have been, but you can make music a creative outlet for your personal enjoyment.

Repeat this exercise for the young adult and mature adult stages of your life. If you were to learn new lessons today, what would they contain that your previous lessons did not allow? In performing this analysis, look at the following areas of life: family, sexuality, denial, service, friends, money, religion, self-esteem, career, men/women, armed forces, food, school, rituals, sacrifice, death.

Let your spiritual guide help you complete your development.

Dysfunctional qualities usually result from incomplete development of some aspect of your life. To address this problem, imagine that you have a spiritual guide who is taking you back in time to explore your unlearned lessons. Remember in *A*

Christmas Carol, when three spirits take Scrooge on a tour of his life? In a similar way, your spiritual guide will present him- or herself to you. Take a moment to close your eyes and visualize your spirit guide now.

Next, ask your parent(s) or other people who were essential to your development to appear. Imagine that you are all going back to times in the past when your development was hindered. You may see yourself playing alone as a child, for example. You feel lonely because no one is paying attention to you. Communicate these feelings, which you were unable to verbalize then (and are still carrying), to your spirit guide and your parent. You might say, "Look at little Timothy over there. He is playing with imaginary friends because you didn't give him any time. He's running into his room now because he's terrified by your screaming. And when the lights go out he's going to talk to his little friends about you." Repeat this process for each painful memory to heal the spirit of your parents, teachers or others who contributed to your lack of development.

Then look at yourself as a teenager and identify painful experiences that have not been communicated and resolved. If a girl was date-raped as a teenager, for example, she may not have told her parents for fear they would hold her responsible and view her with shame. As a result, she has suffered silently for many years and may even be physically sick. Now she can ask her spirit guide to show her parents the emotional pain she endured due to a lack of love and support. By explaining such feelings to your parents, you can forgive them and let go of the past. You will resolve the pain and complete another important lesson.

Remember, the guide is teaching your parents about the pain by showing them what the child is feeling. In effect, you're working on a spiritual level to get to the core of the incomplete parts of your development. You're seeing how your past affected you, and you're allowing yourself to forgive your parents and others who played an important role in your development.

What areas of your life need attention? Are you addressing your essential needs?

Are you ignoring important areas of your life because they appear to be out of your control? You may be afraid that you will feel bad about yourself if you fail at a new endeavor, or you may worry that others will judge you by such failures. Don't simply deny that needs exist in order to avoid dealing with them. If your relationships are unhealthy, for example, you must engage in healthy relationships to grow. Start by learning some lessons from your past relationships. Examine the constructive and destructive aspects of each and ask yourself which essential needs were being met and which were not.

Look at other areas of your life as well, and strive to fulfill your essential needs. Let go of everything else. Once you identify your true needs, it will be easy to walk away from the nonessentials. I've built some beautiful things in my life, including a restaurant, a ranch and a farm, but I let them go the moment they were no longer essential to me. The change came easily because I could break my connection to them when they no longer served my needs.

Clearly our essential needs can change as we progress through life. A 40-year-old spends his day differently than does a 20-year-old because his feelings about mortality change. Few 20-year-olds run in the park, while thousands of 40-year-olds do so because exercise has become more essential to them. It helps them feel younger and healthier and slows down the aging process.

What is essential to your well-being today? What things do you hold onto out of habit, even though they no longer serve an essential function in your life? Focus on attending to your essential needs, and let go of the nonessentials.

How do your perceptions distort reality?

Your perception of the world may prevent you from enjoying life. When your perceptions distort reality, they can affect you more than the event itself. If you are in a beautiful meadow, do you perceive the grandeur of nature or unseen hazards such as snakes and lizards? The danger in letting perceptions overshadow reality is that you lose sight of what is real and important.

What things in your life could be viewed as misdirected perceptions? Which perceptions bother or intimidate you? List the perceptions that limit your happiness and well-being. Try to reassess the situation in a more positive light.

Begin to reconstruct your "real self."

Where does this process begin? First you must accept your imperfections as a part of your being. Then you can identify ways to transform each imperfection and eliminate it from your life. Although few of us like to acknowledge the parts of our lives that do not work, you can only grow by recognizing the weakest part of yourself. One liability can negate many assets. Just as you cannot build the Taj Mahal on a foundation of quicksand and expect it to stand, you cannot expect to change without an honest assessment of your flaws.

Work on one shortcoming at a time. Ask yourself, "How can I convert this imperfection from a weakness to a strength?" Stay with the imperfection until you have resolved it. Don't deny the problem; deal with it. If necessary, get feedback from another person or a support group to help you with the process.

Are you living a role that masks your true self in order to cope?

Many people get caught up in archetypal or culturally prescribed behavior patterns. Some of these include: 1) the predator/aggressor/dominator; 2) the prey/victim/submissive/blamed; 3) the savior/warrior/hero; 4) the magician/illusionist/escape artist. See where these or other roles appear in your life.

The predator needs to conquer, dominate and control, while the prey is a submissive victim who takes blame for everything. The magician seeks to escape reality. Many people, particularly artists, can identify with a need for fantasy and illusion. And saviors, for their part, generally have been hurt in some way. To compensate for the pain, they strive to win favor and praise from others and thereby raise their self-esteem. They want someone else to validate their life when, in fact, this validation must come from within.

You may exhibit various combinations of these behaviors at different times. But these roles can mask your inner self, so be alert to the ways in which they show up in your life.

How do you use control and guilt?

Control itself is neither constructive or destructive. What matters are the reasons behind your use of control. For example, do you try to induce guilt in others when they begin to make positive changes? Suppose your husband makes noticeable improvements in his physical and mental health by joining a health club. If you feel threatened by these changes, you may retaliate by making him feel guilty for spending time away from the family. Similarly you may use guilt as a defense mechanism to avoid making much-needed changes in yourself.

List the control and guilt mechanisms you use, and then examine your reasons for using them. Are your reasons for controlling a situation constructive or destructive? Do you try to improve the situation or do you become vindictive? Do you make someone else feel guilty because you are afraid of change?

Can you separate real needs from conditioned needs?

Learn to distinguish between the things you are conditioned to want and those you truly need. Our conditioned wants are not necessarily bad; in some cases, they may reflect our true needs. But you must separate the fact from the fiction so that you can abandon the conditioned needs that do not represent your true self. For example, you may have been conditioned to believe that living in a luxury apartment is a symbol of success and a key to happiness. When it comes right down to it, though, you would be much happier in a little country home.

Define the boundaries of your inner self.

Be wary of people who try to attack your thoughts and make you think as they do. No one has that right. Your inner self is a place where you can be comfortable. If people try to invade this space, let them know that it's off limits to them.

Make a list of the thoughts you have that are exclusively yours. Then write down the ones that are influenced by others.

If you expressed your real self, what type of confrontation would occur? What would change?

When you begin to identify and express your real needs, sooner or later you will come into conflict with someone. Here is where you must take control by standing up for yourself and continuing to express your inner truth. Consider such confrontations as opportunities for growth. Initially other people may resist the changes you have made, but you must persevere to establish your newfound sense of self.

12

Just Do It

Take control, discover what you want and then let people know that you are ready to share your positive energies.

12

How would you fare if you put your life on trial?

Make a list of people in your life—family members, friends, coworkers, supervisors, religious leaders, teachers—and then describe their opinions of you (based on your perceptions). Assume that your character is on trial. These people will be weighing the good and bad. How do you fare? Where do your weaknesses lie? Is there a consistent misperception? Perhaps they all perceive you as stingy when you see yourself as giving. As your own attorney, how do you defend yourself? If their perceptions are correct and the fault lies within, what can you do to change their perception of you?

What types of circumstances make you feel good or bad?

Look at a typical period of time in your life. Identify the elements that make you feel good and those that make you feel bad. Some of these may include:

- Acceptance
- Security
- Calmness
- Freedom
- Happiness
- Relief
- Relaxation
- Balance
- Words
- Sound
- Taste
- Smell
- Touch
- Other people's behavior

Acceptance

Acceptance creates positive feelings. When people accept you unconditionally, you emote good feelings.

Security

Security also generates a positive response. List the things that make you feel secure, such as selfesteem, love, appreciation or feeling comfortable.

Calmness

Nature creates serenity because it doesn't require anything of you. There's a natural rhythm to listening to the rain on the roof, watching a sunset or sunrise or watching the moonlight on a quiet lake.

Freedom

You will feel free when your life is in control, but you do not have to control others.

Happiness

What makes you feel happy and carefree? Can you get in touch with the inner child? When the child within comes out to play, you forget your troubles and do things just for the sake of doing them. You don't worry about making mistakes. You lighten up and enjoy the moment.

Relief

This feeling usually follows a crisis, when you no longer have to deal with the tension and anxiety created by the situation. The stark contrast of these times makes you appreciate everyday life all the more.

Relaxation

You feel relaxed when you can be yourself and don't have to do anything special, such as when you sleep in on a Sunday morning. The opposite feeling occurs when you try to please others because you are engrossed in projecting an image that you want them to see. You should be able to relax a good part of the time, not just in rare moments.

Balance

Any action or behavior taken to an extreme will adversely affect your sense of well-being. If you exercise excessively or not at all, you are unbalanced. If you eat too much or too little, you're unbalanced. If you cannot express love or you show love to the point of obsession, you're unbalanced.

To achieve balance, then, you must be at peace with who you are. This process requires focus, attention and time spent on self-development. When you identify your excesses and balance them, you will find the time to be a whole and happy person.

Words

Words have the power to offend, control and demean when they are purposely used that way. You may have been conditioned to respond to certain words with submission or anger. It's no accident that the term "boy" was used to address black men. It was meant to dehumanize and disempower them, just as the word "girl" kept women in their place before the advent of the women's liberation movement. People didn't have to treat you like a man if they called you boy, and they didn't have to respect you as an intelligent woman if they called you girl.

Make a list of the words to which you react. You'll be able to view them differently—and maintain control of the situation—if you can hear these words without getting emotionally involved. Try to accept them as just words. Equally important, make a conscious effort to use words that encourage other people. Why not make people feel good about who they are? Think about what it feels like to be on the other end of what you are sharing.

Never gossip. If you have something to say to someone, talk to him or her about it privately. Don't threaten or intimidate, just say what you feel. If someone does something that concerns or displeases you, don't automatically assume that he or she is wrong. Give others an opportunity to explain their side, and you just might see the situation from a different perspective.

Sound

Think of the sounds that make you feel good. Try to surround yourself with these sounds as much as possible.

Taste

Take time to savor the foods that taste good to you. Even if you're having a quick snack or lunch, chew your food slowly and really experience the flavor.

Smell

Pleasant smells provide a great psychological boost. In fact, many hospitals are now trying to foster the healing process by replacing medicinal odors with pleasant aromas.

Touch

The sense of touch is a healthy stimulus. We demonstrate true love when we hold hands or hug. Unfortunately, our society discourages hugging because we characterize it as sexual. In the process, we overlook one of the greatest therapeutic actions available to us in life.

Other people's behavior

Modern society breeds paranoia in many people. But as long as you fear others, you will never be in control of your life. You will feel helpless, rejected, insecure, anxious, controlled, sad, apprehensive, tense and weak. Believe in yourself and know that you can handle any situation.

What causes your life to stagnate?

Have you ever noticed that you tend to rely on the same old excuses—and recycle the same old doubts—when you want to avoid making changes in your life? Suppose that you make excuses not to go out with your friends time after time. By doing so you are purposely sabotaging your chances of meeting new people, even though you later complain that you never meet anyone.

Make a list of your standard excuses and examine them for this type of interference.

How do you compromise your principles to gain acceptance?

Like many people, you may substantially compromise your true needs to gain acceptance from others. In doing so, you make your own needs secondary to those accepted by the person or group from which you want to gain favor. As long as you allow this scenario to continue, you will have to circumvent your needs.

Examine your relationships and the social and professional groups to which you belong. Determine if these relationships interfere with your true needs.

Do you share your best qualities?

What qualities do you have that make your life exciting? These might include the gift of joy, creativity, spontaneity, openness, fellowship or benevolence. Learn to recognize these qualities in yourself and to share them with others. Allow yourself to experience the benefits and deep appreciation that can come from giving a small part of your life to somebody else.

List your best qualities and describe the ways in which you benefit from sharing these characteristics.

Do you focus on the negative?

Many people dwell on what does not work in their lives. They forget that their daily life, for the most part, does indeed work; otherwise they wouldn't be here. They tend to forget the events in life that have fostered their growth and happiness and the moments of true passion. Some people believe they had a terrible childhood, for example, because they allow the bad memories to overshadow the good. As victims of the past, they limit their growth to retaliate against their parents for the things they did not do or the encouragement they did not provide.

List the good things you remember about your childhood. Recall the times your friends and family encouraged, helped and directed you. You will discover a lot more positive instances than you thought. Perhaps your father spent a lot of quality time with you on fishing trips or at ball games while your mother taught you to cook or sew. There's a lot to feel happy and satisfied about when you reflect on positive experiences. By acknowledging these beneficial times, you will appreciate life more than if you allow yourself to be overwhelmed by the negative.

Do you accept other people as they are?

One of the most difficult challenges in life is to allow people to be themselves. Usually we try to make others conform to our perception of what they should be, rather than accept them for who they are and go forward with the relationship. Much time and energy are wasted in relationships due to these minor differences. You must recognize that it's impossible for two people to agree about everything, and then choose your friends according to their overall qualities, not the small details. If you are compatible in the most essential areas—trust, honesty, integrity—this will be the basis of your relationship.

Make a list of your relationships and consider whether or not they meet your fundamental requirements. Can you accept another person for his or her overall characteristics, or are you bogged down in the petty differences?

Do you respect other people's feelings?

Remember that all of your communications should support or enhance your relationships. The way in which you communicate is an active choice. Before you say anything, always ask yourself what it would be like to be on the receiving end of the comment.

It's important to remain aware of this issue in your day-to-day dealings with people. Keep a list of anything you say that's abusive and anything you say to others that you wouldn't like to hear yourself. Then make a commitment to becoming more positive in your communications. You receive the benefits many times over when you give positive input to others.

Do you have trouble making decisions?

Decision-making becomes extremely difficult when you haven't taken the time to define your needs. Perhaps you walk past a discotheque and feel drawn to go in and dance. But another part of you feels uncomfortable about visiting such places alone. You feel conflicted between an inner desire and your conditioning.

When you're in control, on the other hand, decisions become intuitive. There are no contradictions between your inner nature and your outer actions. You have the confidence to be straightforward in fulfilling your needs.

Do you have someone with whom to share your intimate self?

True intimacy means that you share your most private and inner thoughts in the most vulnerable and honest way. It is an unfolding of the heart, mind and spirit. It's important to have such a relationship in your life, where you allow someone to see every aspect of your being. There are no inner secrets or hidden agendas; you can be your true self without fear of being judged, corrected or manipulated in the process.

How can you recover the missing parts of your life?

You need to know what's missing in your life before you can go out and find it. If you have not received unconditional love, for example, then you must find someone who has unconditional love to share. Many people like to think that problems and negative situations will correct themselves, but the fact is they never do. You are the driving force behind change in your life; you are the one who must actively seek to fulfill your needs.

Have faith in yourself and the confidence to know that you can form fulfilling relationships and direct your energies toward fulfillment. Identify what's missing in your life by examining the things that bother you. Forget about blaming others for your problems. It's a wasted effort. Take control, find what you want, and then let people know that you exist and are ready to share your positive energies.

Index by Ann Hall